OECD/G20 Base Erosion and Profit Shifting Project

D1797794

Making Dispute Resolution More Effective – MAP Peer Review Report, Indonesia (Stage 1)

INCLUSIVE FRAMEWORK ON BEPS: ACTION 14

OECD

BETTER POLICIES FOR BETTER LIVES

This document, as well as any data and map included herein, are without prejudice to the status of or sovereignty over any territory, to the delimitation of international frontiers and boundaries and to the name of any territory, city or area.

Please cite this publication as:
OECD (2019), *Making Dispute Resolution More Effective – MAP Peer Review Report, Indonesia (Stage 1): Inclusive Framework on BEPS: Action 14*, OECD/G20 Base Erosion and Profit Shifting Project, OECD Publishing, Paris, *https://doi.org/10.1787/deb42398-en*.

ISBN 978-92-64-32269-1 (print)
ISBN 978-92-64-82045-6 (pdf)

OECD/G20 Base Erosion and Profit Shifting Project
ISSN 2313-2604 (print)
ISSN 2313-2612 (online)

Foreword

The integration of national economies and markets has increased substantially in recent years, putting a strain on the international tax rules, which were designed more than a century ago. Weaknesses in the current rules create opportunities for base erosion and profit shifting (BEPS), requiring bold moves by policy makers to restore confidence in the system and ensure that profits are taxed where economic activities take place and value is created.

Following the release of the report *Addressing Base Erosion and Profit Shifting* in February 2013, OECD and G20 countries adopted a 15-point Action Plan to address BEPS in September 2013. The Action Plan identified 15 actions along three key pillars: introducing coherence in the domestic rules that affect cross-border activities, reinforcing substance requirements in the existing international standards, and improving transparency as well as certainty.

After two years of work, measures in response to the 15 actions were delivered to G20 Leaders in Antalya in November 2015. All the different outputs, including those delivered in an interim form in 2014, were consolidated into a comprehensive package. The BEPS package of measures represents the first substantial renovation of the international tax rules in almost a century. Once the new measures become applicable, it is expected that profits will be reported where the economic activities that generate them are carried out and where value is created. BEPS planning strategies that rely on outdated rules or on poorly co-ordinated domestic measures will be rendered ineffective.

Implementation is now the focus of this work. The BEPS package is designed to be implemented via changes in domestic law and practices, and in tax treaties. With the negotiation of a multilateral instrument (MLI) having been finalised in 2016 to facilitate the implementation of the treaty related BEPS measures, over 85 jurisdictions are covered by the MLI. The entry into force of the MLI on 1 July 2018 paves the way for swift implementation of the treaty related measures. OECD and G20 countries also agreed to continue to work together to ensure a consistent and co-ordinated implementation of the BEPS recommendations and to make the project more inclusive. Globalisation requires that global solutions and a global dialogue be established which go beyond OECD and G20 countries.

A better understanding of how the BEPS recommendations are implemented in practice could reduce misunderstandings and disputes between governments. Greater focus on implementation and tax administration should therefore be mutually beneficial to governments and business. Proposed improvements to data and analysis will help support ongoing evaluation of the quantitative impact of BEPS, as well as evaluating the impact of the countermeasures developed under the BEPS Project.

As a result, the OECD established the OECD/G20 Inclusive Framework on BEPS (Inclusive Framework), bringing all interested and committed countries and jurisdictions on an equal footing in the Committee on Fiscal Affairs and all its subsidiary bodies. The

Inclusive Framework, which already has more than 135 members, is monitoring and peer reviewing the implementation of the minimum standards as well as completing the work on standard setting to address BEPS issues. In addition to BEPS members, other international organisations and regional tax bodies are involved in the work of the Inclusive Framework, which also consults business and the civil society on its different work streams.

This report was approved by the Inclusive Framework on 9 August 2019 and prepared for publication by the OECD Secretariat.

Table of contents

Figures

Abbreviations and acronyms

APA	Advance Pricing Arrangement
FTA	Forum on Tax Administration
MAP	Mutual Agreement Procedure
OECD	Organisation for Economic Co-operation and Development

Executive summary

Indonesia has a relatively large tax treaty network with over 70 tax treaties. Indonesia has an established MAP programme and has modest experience with resolving MAP cases. It has a modest MAP inventory, with a modest number of new cases submitted each year and 59 cases pending on 31 December 2018. Of these cases, 63% concern allocation/attribution cases. Overall Indonesia meets the majority of the elements of the Action 14 Minimum Standard. Where it has deficiencies, Indonesia is working to address some of them.

All of Indonesia's tax treaties contain a provision relating to MAP. Those treaties generally follow paragraphs 1 through 3 of Article 25 of the *Model Tax Convention on Income and Capital 2017* (OECD, 2017). Its treaty network is partly consistent with the requirements of the Action 14 Minimum Standard, except mainly for the fact that:

- Almost 75% of its tax treaties neither contain a provision stating that mutual agreements shall be implemented notwithstanding any time limits in domestic law (which is required under Article 25(2), second sentence), nor the alternative provisions for Article 9(1) and Article 7(2) to set a time limit for making transfer pricing adjustments

- More than 40% of its tax treaties do not contain the equivalent of Article 25(1), second sentence, of the OECD Model Tax Convention (OECD, 2015), as the timeline to file a MAP request is shorter than three years from the first notification of the action resulting in taxation not in accordance with the provision of the tax treaty.

In order to be fully compliant with all four key areas of an effective dispute resolution mechanism under the Action 14 Minimum Standard, Indonesia needs to amend and update a significant number of its tax treaties. In this respect, Indonesia signed the Multilateral Instrument, through which a number of its tax treaties will potentially be modified to fulfil the requirements under the Action 14 Minimum Standard. Where treaties will not be modified, upon entry into force of this Multilateral Instrument for the treaties concerned, Indonesia reported that it intends to update all of its tax treaties via bilateral negotiations to be compliant with the requirements under the Action 14 Minimum Standard, but it has not yet put in place a plan in relation hereto.

Indonesia does not meet the Action 14 Minimum Standard concerning the prevention of disputes. It has in place a bilateral APA programme, but this programme does not necessarily allow roll-back of bilateral APAs in all appropriate cases.

Indonesia meets some of the requirements regarding the availability and access to MAP under the Action 14 Minimum Standard. It provides access to MAP in eligible cases. However, access to MAP will be denied for cases where domestic courts have already rendered a decision on the same issues for which a MAP request was submitted, but also where such court decision regards the same taxpayer for the same fiscal year with regard to the same tax assessment, but is not related to an issue for which a MAP request was submitted. Furthermore, Indonesia requests that taxpayers file a MAP request at the level of the treaty partner for adjustments made by Indonesia, which is contrary to the requirements under Article 25(1) of the OECD Model Tax Convention. Indonesia has in place a documented bilateral consultation and notification process for those situations in which its competent authority considers the objection raised by taxpayers in a MAP request as not justified. Indonesia also has clear and comprehensive guidance on the availability of MAP and how it applies this procedure in practice.

Concerning the average time needed to close MAP cases, the MAP statistics for Indonesia for the period 2016-18 are as follows:

2016-18	Opening inventory 1/1/2016	Cases started	Cases closed	End inventory 31/12/2018	Average time to close cases (in months)*
Attribution/allocation cases	23	40	26	37	27.25
Other cases	45	23	46	22	22.18
Total	68	63	72	59	24.00

*The average time taken for resolving MAP cases for post-2015 cases follows the MAP Statistics Reporting Framework. For computing the average time taken for resolving pre-2016 MAP cases Indonesia used as a start date one week from the date of notification by the competent authority that receives the MAP request from the taxpayer or five weeks from the receipt of the taxpayer's MAP request, whichever is the earlier date; and as an end date the date of an official communication from the competent authority to inform the taxpayer of the outcome of its MAP request.

The number of cases Indonesia closed in the period 2016-18 is more than the number of all new cases started in those years. Its MAP inventory as per 31 December 2018 decreased as compared to its inventory as per 1 January 2016. During these years, MAP cases were closed on average within a timeframe of 24 months (which is the pursued average for closing MAP cases received on or after 1 January 2016), as the average time necessary was equal to 24 months. However, for attribution/allocation cases the average was above 24 months, namely 27.25 months. In addition, a number of peers experienced difficulties in effectively scheduling face-to-face meetings with Indonesia's competent authority, as also obtaining position papers in due time containing sufficient information and analysis on the case under review, as well as receiving responses to position papers and communication on pending MAP cases.

Furthermore, Indonesia meets all the other requirements under the Action 14 Minimum Standard in relation to the resolution of MAP cases. Indonesia's competent authority operates fully independently from the audit function of the tax authorities and the performance indicators used are appropriate to perform the MAP function.

Lastly, Indonesia does not entirely meet the Action 14 Minimum Standard as regards the implementation of MAP agreements. Indonesia monitors the implementation of MAP agreements and most peers raised no issues regarding the implementation throughout the peer review process. Indonesia has a domestic statute of limitation for implementation of MAP agreements, for which there is a risk that such agreements cannot be implemented where the applicable tax treaty does not contain the equivalent of Article 25(2), second sentence, of the OECD Model Tax Convention. In this respect, the outcome of the peer review shows that this domestic statute of limitation may also be applied even if the second sentence is contained in the treaty, but only for cases where the adjustment was made at the level of the treaty partner.

References

OECD (2015), *Model Tax Convention on Income and on Capital 2014 (Full Version)*, OECD Publishing, Paris, https://dx.doi.org/10.1787/9789264239081-en.

OECD (2017), *Model Tax Convention on Income and on Capital 2017 (Full Version)*, OECD Publishing, Paris, https://dx.doi.org/10.1787/g2g972ee-en.

Introduction

Available mechanisms in Indonesia to resolve tax treaty-related disputes

Indonesia has entered into 72 tax treaties on income (and/or capital), 68 of which are in force.[1] These 72 treaties are being applied to an equal number of jurisdictions. All of these treaties provide for a mutual agreement procedure for resolving disputes on the interpretation and application of the provisions of the tax treaty. In addition, one of the 72 treaties provides for an arbitration procedure as a final stage to the mutual agreement procedure.[2]

In Indonesia, the competent authority function to conduct MAP is assigned to the Minister of Finance, which has delegated it, pursuant to Article 57(1) of Government Regulation No. 74 (2011), to the Director General of Taxes. Since April 2016, it is the International Tax Dispute Prevention and Resolution section within the Directorate of International Taxation that handles MAP and APA cases. This directorate operates directly under the Director General of Taxes and currently employs 31 employees that exclusively handle MAP cases.

Indonesia issued several rules, guidelines and procedures on the governance and administration of the mutual agreement procedure ("**MAP**"). The basis hereof is the Government Regulation No. 74/2011, which in Article 59 stipulates that further provisions regarding the mutual agreement procedure shall be stipulated by means of a regulation by the Minister of Finance. On 22 December 2014 the Minister of Finance Regulation No. 240/PMK.3/2014 was issued, which is available at (in English):

https://www.pajak.go.id/sites/default/files/2019-03/PMK-240-2014%20%28EN%29.pdf

Further to the above, Indonesia also established a dedicated webpage containing information on its APA and MAP programme and which is available at:

www.pajak.go.id/apa-map

Recent developments in Indonesia

Indonesia reported it is currently conducting tax treaty negotiations with Ecuador and other jurisdictions. Indonesia has recently signed a new treaty with Cambodia (2017), which has not yet entered into force.

Furthermore, on 7 June 2017, Indonesia signed the Multilateral Convention to Implement Tax Treaty Related Measures to Prevent Base Erosion and Profit Shifting ("**Multilateral Instrument**"), to adopt, where necessary, modifications to the MAP article under its tax treaties with a view to be compliant with the Action 14 Minimum Standard in respect of all the relevant tax treaties. Where treaties will not be modified by the Multilateral Instrument, Indonesia reported that it strives updating them through future bilateral negotiations. Indonesia, however, has not put in place a specific plan for such negotiations.

With the signing of the Multilateral Instrument, Indonesia also submitted its list of notifications and reservations to that instrument.[3] In relation to the Action 14 Minimum Standard, Indonesia reserved, pursuant to Article 16(5)(a), the right not to apply Article 16(1) of the Multilateral Instrument (concerning the mutual agreement procedure) that modifies existing treaties to allow the submission of a MAP request to the competent authorities of either contracting state.[4] This reservation is in line with the requirements of the Action 14 Minimum Standard.

Basis for the peer review process

The peer review process entails an evaluation of Indonesia's implementation of the Action 14 Minimum Standard through an analysis of its legal and administrative framework relating to the mutual agreement procedure, as governed by its tax treaties, domestic legislation and regulations, as well as its MAP programme guidance (if any) and the practical application of that framework. The review process performed is desk-based and conducted through specific questionnaires completed by Indonesia, its peers and taxpayers. The questionnaires for the peer review process were sent to Indonesia and the peers on 31 December 2018.

The period for evaluating Indonesia's implementation of the Action 14 Minimum Standard ranges from 1 January 2016 to 31 December 2018 ("**Review Period**"). In addition to the assessment on its compliance with the Action 14 Minimum Standard, Indonesia also asked for peer input on best practices. Furthermore, this report may depict some recent developments that have occurred after the Review Period, which at this stage will not impact the assessment of Indonesia's implementation of this minimum standard. In the update of this report, being stage 2 of the peer review process, these recent developments will be taken into account in the assessment and, if necessary, the conclusions contained in this report will be amended accordingly.

For the purpose of this report and the statistics below, in assessing whether Indonesia is compliant with the elements of the Action 14 Minimum Standard that relate to a specific treaty provision, the newly negotiated treaties or the treaties as modified by a protocol, as described above, were taken into account, even if it concerned a modification or a replacement of an existing treaty. Reference is made to Annex A for the overview of Indonesia's tax treaties regarding the mutual agreement procedure.

In total 121 peers provided input: Australia, Canada, the People's Republic of China, Denmark, Japan, Korea, the Netherlands, Singapore, Sweden, Switzerland, Turkey and the United States. Out of these 12 peers, eight had MAP cases with Indonesia that started on or after 1 January 2016. These eight peers represents more than 95% of post-2015 MAP cases in Indonesia's inventory that started in 2016-18. Generally, all peers indicated a good and co-operative relationship with Indonesia's competent authority, although some of them experienced administrative difficulties in resolving MAP cases in a timely and effective manner.

Indonesia provided informative answers in its questionnaire, which was submitted on time. Indonesia was responsive the course of the drafting of the peer review report, and provided further clarity where necessary. In addition, Indonesia provided the following information:

- MAP profile[5]

- MAP statistics[6] according to the MAP Statistics Reporting Framework (see below).

Finally, Indonesia is a member of the FTA MAP Forum and has shown co-operation during the peer review process.

Overview of MAP caseload in Indonesia

The analysis of the Indonesia's MAP caseload relates to the period starting on 1 January 2016 and ending on 31 December 2018 ("**Statistics Reporting Period**"). According to the statistics provided by Indonesia, its MAP caseload during this period was as follows:

2016-18	Opening inventory 1/1/2016	Cases started	Cases closed	End inventory 31/12/2017
Attribution/allocation cases	23	40	26	37
Other cases	45	23	46	22
Total	68	63	72	59

General outline of the peer review report

This report includes an evaluation of Indonesia's implementation of the Action 14 Minimum Standard. The report comprises the following four sections:

A. Preventing disputes

B. Availability and access to MAP

C. Resolution of MAP cases

D. Implementation of MAP agreements.

Each of these sections is divided into elements of the Action 14 Minimum Standard, as described in the terms of reference to monitor and review the implementing of the BEPS Action 14 Minimum Standard to make dispute resolution mechanisms more effective ("**Terms of Reference**").[7] Apart from analysing Indonesia's legal framework and its administrative practice, the report also incorporates peer input and responses to such input by Indonesia. Furthermore, the report depicts the changes adopted and plans shared by Indonesia to implement elements of the Action 14 Minimum Standard where relevant. The conclusion of each element identifies areas for improvement (if any) and provides for recommendations how the specific area for improvement should be addressed.

The objective of the Action 14 Minimum Standard is to make dispute resolution mechanisms more effective and concerns a continuous effort. Therefore, this peer review report includes recommendations that Indonesia continues to act in accordance with a given element of the Action 14 Minimum Standard, even if there is no area for improvement for this specific element.

Notes

1. The tax treaties Indonesia has entered into are available at: http://treaty.kemlu.go.id/. The treaties that are signed but have not yet entered into force are with Cambodia (2017), Myanmar (2003), Tajikistan (2003) and Zimbabwe (2001). These treaties are taken into account in the analysis. Reference is made to Annex A for the overview of Indonesia's tax treaties concerning the mutual agreement procedure.

2. This concerns the treaty with Mexico.

3. Available at: www.oecd.org/tax/treaties/beps-mli-position-indonesia.pdf.

4. This reservation on Article 16 – Mutual Agreement Procedure reads: "Pursuant to Article 16(5)(a) of the Convention, Indonesia reserves the right for the first sentence of Article 16(1) not to apply to its Covered Tax Agreements on the basis that it intends to meet the minimum standard for improving dispute resolution under the OECD/G20 BEPS Package by ensuring that under each of its Covered Tax Agreements (other than a Covered Tax Agreement that permits a person to present a case to the competent authority of either Contracting Jurisdiction), where a person considers that the actions of one or both of the Contracting Jurisdictions result or will result for that person in taxation not in accordance with the provisions of the Covered Tax Agreement, irrespective of the remedies provided by the domestic law of those Contracting Jurisdictions, that person may present the case to the competent authority of the Contracting Jurisdiction of which the person is a resident or, if the case presented by that person comes under a provision of a Covered Tax Agreement relating to non-discrimination based on nationality, to that of the Contracting Jurisdiction of which that person is a national; and the competent authority of that Contracting Jurisdiction will implement a bilateral notification or consultation process with the competent authority of the other Contracting Jurisdiction for cases in which the competent authority to which the mutual agreement procedure case was presented does not consider the taxpayer's objection to be justified".

5. Available at www.oecd.org/tax/dispute/Indonesia-Dispute-Resolution-Profile.pdf.

6. The 2016-18 MAP statistics of Indonesia are shown in Annex B and C of this report.

7. Terms of reference to monitor and review the implementing of the BEPS Action 14 Minimum Standard to make dispute resolution mechanisms more effective. Available at: www.oecd.org/tax/beps/beps-action-14-on-more-effective-dispute-resolution-peer-review-documents.pdf.

Part A

Preventing disputes

[A.1] Include Article 25(3), first sentence, of the OECD Model Tax Convention in tax treaties

> Jurisdictions should ensure that their tax treaties contain a provision which requires the competent authority of their jurisdiction to endeavour to resolve by mutual agreement any difficulties or doubts arising as to the interpretation or application of their tax treaties.

1.   Cases may arise concerning the interpretation or the application of tax treaties that do not necessarily relate to individual cases, but are more of a general nature. Inclusion of the first sentence of Article 25(3) of the OECD Model Tax Convention (OECD, 2017a) in tax treaties invites and authorises competent authorities to solve these cases, which may avoid submission of MAP requests and/or future disputes from arising, and which may reinforce the consistent bilateral application of tax treaties.

Current situation of Indonesia's tax treaties

2.   Out of Indonesia's 72 tax treaties, 69 contain a provision that is equivalent to Article 25(3), first sentence, of the OECD Model Tax Convention requiring their competent authority to endeavour to resolve by mutual agreement any difficulties or doubts arising as to the interpretation or application of the tax treaty. Of the remaining three treaties, one does not contain the term "interpretation" and two do not contain the terms "doubts" and "interpretation". For this reason, these three treaties are considered not contain the equivalent of Article 25(3), first sentence, of the OECD Model Tax Convention.

3.   Indonesia reported that where the applicable treaties do not contain the equivalent of Article 25(3), first sentence, of the OECD Model Tax Convention, this does not obstruct its competent authority to enter into MAP agreements of a general concerning the interpretation or the application of tax treaties. Indonesia further specified that for the treaties identified above not containing such equivalent, it has treated discussions of MAP cases of a general nature in the same manner as the treaties that do contain such equivalent.

4.   In view of the above, Article 12 of Regulation 240/PMC.03/2014 stipulates that the Director General of Taxes can request for the initiation of a MAP process relating to issues that are deemed necessary, which *inter alia* concerns interpretation of a certain treaty provision that is necessary for the implementation of the treaty.

Anticipated modifications

Multilateral Instrument

5.   Indonesia signed the Multilateral Instrument. Article 16(4)(c)(i) of that instrument stipulates that Article 16(3), first sentence – containing the equivalent of Article 25(3), first sentence, of the OECD Model Tax Convention – will apply in the absence of a provision in tax treaties that is equivalent to Article 25(3), first sentence, of the OECD Model Tax Convention. In other words, in the absence of this equivalent, Article 16(4)(c)(i) of the Multilateral Instrument will modify the applicable tax treaty to include such equivalent. However, this shall only apply if both contracting parties to the applicable tax treaty have listed this treaty as a covered tax agreement under the Multilateral Instrument and insofar as both notified, pursuant to Article 16(6)(d)(i), the depositary that this treaty does not contain the equivalent of Article 25(3), first sentence, of the OECD Model Tax Convention.

6.   In regard of the three tax treaties identified above that are considered not to contain the equivalent of Article 25(3), first sentence, of the OECD Model Tax Convention, Indonesia listed all of them as a covered tax agreement under the Multilateral Instrument, but for none of them did it make, pursuant to Article 16(6)(d)(i), a notification that they do not contain a provision described in Article 16(4)(c)(i). Therefore, at this stage, none of the three tax treaties identified above will be modified by the Multilateral Instrument to include the equivalent of Article 25(3), first sentence, of the OECD Model Tax Convention.

Bilateral modifications

7.   Indonesia reported that for the three tax treaties identified above that it will modify its notifications under Article 16(6)(d)(i) of the Multilateral Instrument to include these treaties. If done so, the expected impact hereof would be that two of these treaties will be modified by that instrument. For the third treaty there would be no effect, as the relevant treaty partner is not a signatory to the Multilateral Instrument. For this treaty Indonesia further reported that it intends to update it via bilateral negotiations with a view to be compliant with element A.1. Indonesia, however, has not put in place a specific plan for such negotiations nor has it taken any actions to that effect. Regardless, Indonesia indicated it will seek to include Article 25(3), first sentence, of the OECD Model Tax Convention in all of its future tax treaties.

Peer input

8.   Nearly all of the peers that provided input indicated that their treaty with Indonesia meets the requirement under element A.1, which conforms with the above analysis. For the three treaties identified above that do not contain the equivalent of Article 25(3), first sentence, of the OECD Model Tax Convention, two of the relevant peers provided input, one of which indicated that its treaty does not contain such equivalent. The second peer stated that its treaty meets the requirements under the Action 14 Minimum Standard, which does not conform with the above analysis.

Conclusion

	Areas for improvement	Recommendations
[A.1]	Three out of 72 tax treaties do not contain a provision that is equivalent to Article 25(3), first sentence, of the OECD Model Tax Convention. While currently none of these three treaties will be modified by the Multilateral Instrument to include the required provision, such effect is anticipated for two of these three treaties when notifications under that instrument are modified.	Indonesia should as quickly as possible follow its stated intention and modify its notifications under the Multilateral Instrument and subsequently ratify that instrument to incorporate the equivalent of Article 25(3), first sentence, of the OECD Model Tax Convention in two of the three treaties that currently do not contain such equivalent and that will be modified by the Multilateral Instrument upon its entry into force for the treaty concerned.
		For the remaining treaty that will not be modified by the Multilateral Instrument to include the equivalent of Article 25(2), second sentence, of the OECD Model Tax Convention following its entry into force, Indonesia should request the inclusion of the required provision via bilateral negotiations.
		To this end, Indonesia should put a plan in place on how it envisages updating this treaty to include the required provision.
		In addition, Indonesia should maintain its stated intention to include the required provision in all future tax treaties.

[A.2] Provide roll-back of bilateral APAs in appropriate cases

> Jurisdictions with bilateral advance pricing arrangement ("APA") programmes should provide for the roll-back of APAs in appropriate cases, subject to the applicable time limits (such as statutes of limitation for assessment) where the relevant facts and circumstances in the earlier tax years are the same and subject to the verification of these facts and circumstances on audit.

9.   An APA is an arrangement that determines, in advance of controlled transactions, an appropriate set of criteria (e.g. method, comparables and appropriate adjustment thereto, critical assumptions as to future events) for the determination of the transfer pricing for those transactions over a fixed period of time.[1] The methodology to be applied prospectively under a bilateral or multilateral APA may be relevant in determining the treatment of comparable controlled transactions in previous filed years. The "roll-back" of an APA to these previous filed years may be helpful to prevent or resolve potential transfer pricing disputes.

Indonesia's APA programme

10.   Indonesia reported that it has introduced an APA programme in 2010, under which it is allowed to enter into unilateral and bilateral APAs. The legal basis of this programme is Article 32A of Law No. 7 of 1983 concerning Income Tax Law as amended by Law No. 36 of 2008 and the MAP provision of the relevant tax treaty. Article 32A stipulates that Indonesia's competent authority is authorised to enter into agreements with treaty partners to determine the transfer price between associated enterprises. The authority competent to handle APA cases is, pursuant to Article 58(1) of Regulation No. 74 (2011), the Director General of Taxes of the Ministry of Finance.[2]

11.   Article 58 of the Government Regulation No. 74/2011 concerning Taxation Rights and Obligations Fulfilment Procedure also includes rules relating to Indonesia's APA programme. This provision, for example, stipulates that an APAs shall bind the tax administration and

the taxpayer during the period the APA applies and that the tax administration cannot make adjustments on matters already agreed in the APA.

12.   Further to the above, Indonesia issued Regulation No. 7/PMK.03/2015 of 12 January 2015.[3] Article 2(2) of this regulation prescribes that taxpayers may submit an APA application, provided that they have operated business activities in Indonesia for at least three years. As to the period that can be covered by an APA, Article 4 stipulates that this is for a maximum of three fiscal years in case of an unilateral APA and a maximum of four fiscal years in case of a bilateral APA. Furthermore, this regulation contains information on Indonesia's APA programme and how its runs that programme in practice. In particular this concerns information on: (i) which government authority is competent for handling APA requests, (ii) what an APA is and what the requirements for obtaining an APA are, (iii) by whom they can be requested, (iv) what steps have to be followed in the process, (v) a detailed list of information to be included in an APA request, (vi) time limits for the submission of an APA request, (vii) the implementation of an APA and (viii) the possibility to renew an APA.

13.   Further to the above, Indonesia also includes information on its APA programme on the website of the Ministry of Finance.[4] This website reproduces the information included in Regulation No. 7/PMK.03/2015. It is there stated that the information contained on the website should be read in conjunction with Regulation No. 7/PMK.03/2015.

14.   With regard to the timing of the submission of APA requests, Articles 6 and 7 of the APA regulation requires taxpayers to submit a written pre-lodgement request to start the process, whereby such a request should be filed no later than six months before the beginning of the fiscal year covered by the APA.

Roll-back of bilateral APAs

15.   Indonesia reported that its APA programme currently does not provide for roll-back of bilateral APAs. As described in paragraph 14 above, the taxpayer is required to submit a pre-lodgement request no later than six months before the covered tax year to start the APA process, which would rule out a roll-back of bilateral APAs.

16.   Indonesia, however, also reported that Article 19(2) of Regulation No. 7/PMK.03/2015 states that bilateral APAs shall be implemented in accordance with the result of a MAP agreement, as it is the MAP provision under a tax treaty that constitute the legal basis for entering into bilateral APAs. In that regard, Indonesia stated that this could be construed that a roll-back can be granted under the current APA and MAP regulations.[5] To this Indonesia added that conditions and prerequisites for granting roll-back are not explicitly stated in the MAP guidance or APA regulates, and taxpayers may not immediately be aware of the possibility of the provision of roll-back.

Practical application of roll-back of bilateral APAs

17.   The website of Indonesia's tax administration includes statistics on unilateral and bilateral APAs.[6] In this respect, Indonesia reported the following statistics concerning the number of bilateral APA cases:

Year	Beginning inventory	Number of APAs requested	Number of APAs concluded	Ending inventory
2016	11	13	3	21
2017	21	1	2	20
2018	20	13	4	29

18.   Regarding these statistics, Indonesia reported that none of these APA request concerned a request for a roll-back of bilateral APAs. While Indonesia clarified that it has granted roll-backs, the relevant agreement hereto was concluded before 2016.

Peer input

19.   Of the peers that provided input, five indicated they have no bilateral APA cases with Indonesia and/or also no cases concerning the roll-back of bilateral APAs. Furthermore, three peers reported positive experiences in handling roll-back requests with Indonesia. One peer reported that it has received a request for roll-back in respect of one APA case since 1 January 2016 and that Indonesia provided roll-back. Another peer also reported that it has received one roll-back request and that Indonesia was open to negotiate. The third peer experienced that the outcome of a bilateral APA would sometimes be applied to a previous year, for which it considered that granting roll-back of bilateral APAs to previous tax years does not seem to be a problem.

20.   Further to the above, three peers voiced a different input. One of these peers mentioned that since 1 January 2016 it has received three requests for a bilateral APA concerning Indonesia, but that none of them concerned a roll-back as Indonesia does not allow a roll-back due to domestic legal constraints. This input was echoed by that two other peers, who mentioned that since 1 January 2016 their competent authorities have received one request for a roll-back of a bilateral APA. For this case, the peer mentioned that Indonesia's competent authority has been presenting its firm position not to allow roll-back due to lack of a provision in its relevant domestic legislation, and the case is still under negotiation.

21.   To this particular input Indonesia responded and stated that while it does not allow for a roll-back in its existing APA programme, but that it has a solid precedence to grant roll-back by applying the MAP agreement to previous years, provided that the taxpayer officially requested the roll-back. The relevant peer whose input was reflected in paragraph 20 above gave a reaction and mentioned it is not aware of such a precedence nor was it involved in the relevant case. In fact, the peer stressed that while one taxpayer officially requested a roll-back of a bilateral APA with the peer's competent authority, in the minutes of a face-to-face meeting between their competent authorities it is clearly stated that because of domestic regulations, it is not possible to grant roll-back of bilateral APAs.

Anticipated modifications

22.   Indonesia reported that it intends to change its APA programme by amending regulation No. 7/PMK.03/2015. These changes pertain to: (i) clarifying that roll-back of unilateral and bilateral APAs are possible, (ii) simplifying procedures for obtaining APAs and preparation of standardised forms for submission of APA requests, (iii) introducing certainty regarding the to be applied time limits in each phase of the process of obtaining an APA and (iv) improving the process within Indonesia's competent authority regarding the APA programme.

Conclusion

	Areas for improvement	Recommendations
[A.2]	Roll-back of bilateral APAs is not always available in appropriate cases and there are no clear rules available on whether such roll-backs are possible and, if so, upon what conditions.	Indonesia should follow up on its stated intention and amend regulation No. 7/PMK.03/2015 to clarify that roll-back of bilateral APAs are possible. It should in practice also allow for roll-back of bilateral APAs in all appropriate cases.

Notes

1. This description of an APA based on the definition of an APA in the OECD Transfer Pricing Guidelines (OECD, 2017b) for Multinational Enterprises and Tax Administrations.

2. The Government Regulation No. 74/2011 concerning Taxation Rights and Obligations Fulfilment Procedure is available at: https://www.pajak.go.id/sites/default/files/2019-03/PP-74-2011%20%28EN%29.pdf.

3. Available in English at: https://www.pajak.go.id/sites/default/files/2019-03/PMK-7-2015%20%28EN%29.pdf.

4. Available at: http://pajak.go.id/apa-map.

5. See also http://pajak.go.id/apa-map, where it is clarified that roll-back of bilateral APAs is possible provided that the facts and circumstances of the case are the same as for the fiscal years to which the APA applies. The way to obtain a roll-back is via the MAP process.

6. Available at: http://pajak.go.id/apa-map.

References

OECD (2017a), *Model Tax Convention on Income and on Capital 2017 (Full Version)*, OECD Publishing, Paris, https://dx.doi.org/10.1787/g2g972ee-en.

OECD (2017b), *OECD Transfer Pricing Guidelines for Multinational Enterprises and Tax Administrations 2017*, https://dx.doi.org/10.1787/tpg-2017-en.

Part B

Availability and access to MAP

[B.1]   Include Article 25(1) of the OECD Model Tax Convention in tax treaties

> Jurisdictions should ensure that their tax treaties contain a MAP provision which provides that when the taxpayer considers that the actions of one or both of the Contracting Parties result or will result for the taxpayer in taxation not in accordance with the provisions of the tax treaty, the taxpayer, may irrespective of the remedies provided by the domestic law of those Contracting Parties, make a request for MAP assistance, and that the taxpayer can present the request within a period of no less than three years from the first notification of the action resulting in taxation not in accordance with the provisions of the tax treaty.

23.   For resolving cases of taxation not in accordance with the provisions of the tax treaty, it is necessary that tax treaties include a provision allowing taxpayers to request a mutual agreement procedure and that this procedure can be requested irrespective of the remedies provided by the domestic law of the treaty partners. In addition, to provide certainty to taxpayers and competent authorities on the availability of the mutual agreement procedure, a minimum period of three years for submission of a MAP request, beginning on the date of the first notification of the action resulting in taxation not in accordance with the provisions of the tax treaty, is the baseline.

Current situation of Indonesia's tax treaties

Inclusion of Article 25(1), first sentence of the OECD Model Tax Convention

24.   Out of Indonesia's 72 tax treaties, 59 contain a provision that is equivalent to Article 25(1), first sentence, of the OECD Model Tax Convention (OECD, 2017) as it read prior to the adoption of the *Making Dispute Resolution Mechanisms More Effective, Action 14 – 2015 Final Report* (Action 14 Final Report, OECD, 2015a), allowing taxpayers to submit a MAP request to the competent authority of the state in which they are resident when they consider that the actions of one or both of the treaty partners result or will result for the taxpayer in taxation not in accordance with the provisions of the tax treaty and that can be requested irrespective of the remedies provided by domestic law of either state. In addition, none of Indonesia's tax treaties contains a provision equivalent to Article 25(1), first sentence, of the OECD Model Tax Convention (OECD, 2015b), as changed by the Action 14 final report and allowing taxpayers to submit a MAP request to the competent authority of either state.

25.   The remaining 13 tax treaties can be categorised as follows:

Provision	Number of tax treaties
A variation of Article 25(1), first sentence, of the OECD Model Tax Convention as it read prior to the adoption of the Action 14 final report, whereby taxpayers can only submit a MAP request to the competent authority of the contracting state of which they are resident.	12
A variation of Article 25(1), first sentence, of the OECD Model Tax Convention as it read prior to the adoption of the Action 14 final report, whereby taxpayers can only submit a MAP request to the competent authority of the contracting state of which they are resident and whereby the taxpayer can pursuant to a protocol provision not submit a MAP request irrespective of domestic available remedies.	1

26.   The 12 treaties mentioned in the first row of the table are considered not to have the full equivalent of Article 25(1), first sentence, of the OECD Model Tax Convention as it read prior to the adoption of the Action 14 final report, since taxpayers are not allowed to submit a MAP request in the state of which they are a national where the case comes under the non-discrimination article. However, for the following reasons 11 of those12 treaties are considered to be in line with this part of element B.1:

- the relevant tax treaty does not contain a non-discrimination provision and only applies to residents of one of the states (two treaties)

- the non-discrimination provision of the relevant tax treaty only covers nationals that are resident of one of the contracting states. Therefore, it is logical to only allow for the submission of MAP requests to the state of which the taxpayer is a resident (nine treaties).

27.   For the remaining treaty, the non-discrimination provision is almost identical to Article 24(1) of the OECD Model Tax Convention and applies both to nationals that are and are not resident of one of the contracting states. The omission of the full text of Article 25(1), first sentence, of the OECD Model Tax Convention is therefore not clarified by the absence of or a limited scope of the non-discrimination provision, following which it is considered not to be in line with this part of element B.1.

28.   The treaty in the second row of the table incorporates a provision in the protocol to this treaty, which reads:

With reference to paragraph 1 of Article 25, the expression "notwithstanding the remedies provided by the national laws" means that the mutual agreement procedure is not alternative with the national contentious proceedings which shall be, in any case, preventively initiated, when the claim is related with an assessment of the taxes not in accordance with this agreement.

29.   As pursuant to this provision a domestic procedure has to be initiated concomitantly to the initiation of the mutual agreement procedure, a MAP request can in practice thus not be submitted irrespective of the remedies provided by the domestic law. This treaty is therefore also considered not to be in line with this part of element B.1.

30.   In view of this treaty, Indonesia commented that it treats this treaty as being equivalent to Article 25(1), first sentence, of the OECD Model Tax Convention, regardless of this protocol provision.

Inclusion of Article 25(1), second sentence of the OECD Model Tax Convention

31.   Out of Indonesia's 72 tax treaties, 35 contain a provision that is equivalent to Article 25(1), second sentence, of the OECD Model Tax Convention allowing taxpayers to submit a MAP request within a period of no less than three years from the first notification

of the action resulting in taxation not in accordance with the provisions of the particular tax treaty.

32.   The remaining 37 tax treaties that do not contain such provision can be categorised as follows:

Provision	Number of tax treaties
No filing period for a MAP request	4
Filing period less than 3 years for a MAP request (2 years)	33

Practical application

Article 25(1), first sentence, of the OECD Model Tax Convention

(I) Interaction between MAP and domestic remedies

33.   As noted in paragraph 28 and 29 above, in all but one of Indonesia's tax treaties taxpayers can file a MAP request irrespective of domestic remedies. In this respect, Indonesia reported that taxpayers are allowed to file a MAP request and at the same time initiate domestic remedies. However, the MAP proceedings would be ended once domestic courts have issued a ruling on the case or where a hearing on the case has been finalised by the tax court. Indonesia clarified that it is because taxpayers or the tax administration could not present additional facts to the court after the hearing process is finalised, and the court decision is delivered on that basis. In such a situation, the further pursuance of the MAP case would in Indonesia's view become ineffective and could not result in a positive outcome to affect the court decision. Furthermore, if a domestic court has already rendered a decision and the taxpayer would afterwards file a MAP request, Indonesia reported that then access to MAP would be denied.

34.   In this regard, Article 5(1) of the Minister of Finance Regulation No. 240/PMK.03/2014 and Article 57(3) of Regulation No. 74/2011 confirms that taxpayers can file a MAP request at the same time domestic remedies are initiated. Article 5(3) and Article 57(7) respectively also confirm that a MAP request cannot be filed in the event that hearing has been finalised by the tax court for the case for which also a MAP request is filed.[1] In addition, also Article 57(3) of Regulation No. 74/2011 stipulates that the MAP case will be terminated in case domestic court have rendered a decision.[2]

35.   Further to the above, Indonesia clarified that the court process itself does not prevent the taxpayer from accessing MAP until hearings are finalised, and that in practice it could take more than three years from the issuance of a notice of tax assessment before court procedures are finalised. In this respect, Indonesia reported that it will notify its treaty partners of cases pending in court for which also a MAP request is submitted, but that since 1 January 2016 its competent authority has never denied access to MAP due to a court case already being finalised.

36.   Three peers provided input on this subject. One peer pointed to the MAP profile of Indonesia, where it is stated that Indonesia does not proceed MAP discussion when the tax court made a decision. While this peer believes that this is acceptable and reasonable, but only if the court's decision relates to the same issue for which a MAP case is pending. In practice, this peer mentioned that it encountered that Indonesia's competent authority terminated the MAP process after the tax court decision was made on an issue that was not related to the MAP case. The peer clarified that this case was initiated for adjustments made by Indonesia relating to both transfer pricing and local tax issues concerning

the same taxable year. The taxpayer thereby requested a MAP for the transfer pricing adjustments and initiated domestic court procedures for the local tax issues. According to the peer, Indonesia's competent authority expressed the view that the court decision was based on the assumption that the taxpayer had agreed and accepted the transfer pricing adjustment even though the tax court only examined and adjudicated on the local tax issue. On that bases Indonesia's competent authority stated that it was impossible to recalculate the amount of taxes after the court decision had been made and therefore it had to terminate the MAP process. Given this input, this peer believes that the consequence of not being able to proceed with the case in MAP for the transfer pricing adjustment based on a court decision that is irrelevant for the MAP case, is critical and unacceptable for the taxpayer. It also believes that Indonesia's legal and narrow interpretation may limit taxpayers' access to MAP for similar cases, or will cause that taxpayers would only apply for domestic remedies to obtain a full resolution of all issues of the case. In the peer's view, in order to obtain a full resolution in a transfer pricing case, the MAP process needs to be finalised before the court procedures are finalised, or taxpayers should not initiate domestic remedies for local tax issues. The peer concluded that these options are not satisfactory, as they provide incomplete remedies to taxpayers. It also concluded that Indonesia's practice constitutes a de-facto limitation of access to MAP. It therefore suggested that Indonesia should change its policy and continue discussions in MAP on the transfer pricing adjustment, unless the tax court takes a decision for this adjustment.

37.   The second peer reported similar experiences. It mentioned that for attribution/allocation cases its competent authority and that of Indonesia have different views on the interaction between Indonesia's domestic law and the MAP process. For example, Indonesia's competent authority reported it was not able to discuss attribution/allocation cases when taxpayers also initiated appeals with the Indonesia tax court for non-transfer pricing issues.

38.   The third peer reported that seven MAP cases were initiated under its treaty with Indonesia since 1 January 2016. It noted that two of these cases were withdrawn by the taxpayers, for which it understood from these taxpayers that the reason hereof was that domestic court proceedings were about to finalise and they therefore decided to pursue these proceedings over MAP.

39.   Indonesia provided a response to the input given and mentioned that under its Law on General Provision and Tax Procedures, a single tax assessment letter is issued for a fiscal year, which may cover several issues, such as transfer and non-transfer pricing issues. When a taxpayer decides to initiate domestic remedies for the non-transfer pricing issue, the court will decide on this specific issue, but the relevant decision will affect the entire tax assessment (thus including both the transfer pricing and non-transfer pricing issues). Indonesia further clarified that once the court has rendered its decision, there is no possibility for the tax administration to amend the tax assessment, thus also not through the MAP process. To this Indonesia added that both its tax administration and the competent authority do not have the option to intervene or control the process, since the tax court operates independently. In that regard, Indonesia considered that it would not be effective to continue the MAP process after the court has rendered its decision, albeit that in practice it would be able to continue the process, but in that situation Indonesia's competent authority would be the same as the ruling of the court.

40.   Two peers that provided input, reacted to Indonesia's response. The first peer, whose input is reflected in paragraph 36 above, mentioned that the clarification provided by Indonesia does not seem to be in line with the ruling of the tax court. The peer pointed to the fact that upon a request by the taxpayer, the tax court expressed its opinion by stating that the court shall only examine and adjudicate an appeal against an adjustment that is

disputed. Therefore, an adjustment that is not disputed shall not be examined by the court in the appeals process. The peer added that even if Indonesia's clarification was in line with the court's reasoning, this practice and policy would limit taxpayers' access to the MAP process and therefore is not in line with the MAP provision in their mutual tax treaty. Indonesia noted the peer's reaction and mentioned it does understand its concern. It also mentioned that it will take the issue into account in the amendment of its MAP guidance, to clarify that taxpayers have access to MAP irrespective of whether a court rendered a decision. That being said, Indonesia also mentioned that while the court will in the case mentioned only ruled on the issue for which no adjustment was made, the decision affected the whole tax assessment, including an issue for which an adjustment was made.

41. The second peer, whose input is reflected in paragraph 37 above, expressed its appreciation of Indonesia's explanation. It also suggested that because taxpayers and treaty partners may not fully understand the effect of a judicial decision on the MAP process with respect to issues for which an adjustment was made and that was not subject of the court procedure, Indonesia could highlight this effect in its MAP guidance and the guidance on domestic remedies.

42. Taken Indonesia's policy, peer input and responses into consideration it follows that access to MAP will be denied when domestic courts have already rendered a decision on the case for which a MAP request was submitted. Furthermore, such access will also be denied when the court has ruled on an issue that is not subject of MAP discussions, but is included in the same tax assessment as the issue for which a MAP request was submitted. In both instances, Indonesia's policy and practice is contrary to Article 25(1) of the OECD Model Tax Convention, which allows taxpayers to request for the initiation of the MAP process irrespective of domestic remedies. This is further clarified in paragraph 8 of the Commentary to Article 25, which stipulates that the MAP process is clearly a procedure outside of the domestic law. The mere fact of a court decision is not a ground to deny access to MAP, especially as it deprives taxpayers of having the case resolved through the MAP process because the treaty partner may give relief of double taxation.

(II) Access to MAP and the finality of a tax assessment

43. One peer provided input with regard to access to MAP and the finality of a tax assessment. It reported that since 1 January 2016, its competent authority has presented MAP requests it had received to Indonesia's competent authority, which declined to discuss these cases in the MAP process. In 2017, the reason for such refusal was that Indonesia's tax authority had not yet issued any tax assessments for these taxpayers, which in Indonesia's view is required before a case can be dealt with in MAP. The peer further noted that Indonesia's competent authority indicated that it will provide access when such an assessment is issued and that, in the meantime, it would treat the requests as protective MAP requests. This peer takes the position that once a taxpayer has been notified of a potential taxation by Indonesia's tax authority that is not in accordance with the treaty and that is not merely possible but probable, access to MAP should be given regardless of whether a formal assessment has been issued.

44. Indonesia responded by stating that the notification from the local tax offices to taxpayers is merely an administrative letter that does not have any legal effect. Such letter is generally used to seek clarification for some tax issues that the taxpayer may face in its transactions. However, if the taxpayer could clarify those issues based on the facts, Indonesia clarified that there would not be any legal actions taken by the tax administration (including but not limited to audits). In that regard, Indonesia concluded that the issuing of

an administrative letter stand alone would not result in taxation that is not in accordance with the treaty.

45. The peer reacted to this response and stated that in its understanding, which was based on communications with the taxpayer, the taxpayer was under the impression that a tax assessment would directly follow from the issuing of the said letter. In the peer's view, while the letter from itself would not result in taxation that is not in accordance with the provisions of the tax treaty, it may provide evidence that there is a risk that such taxation is probable. In such a situation, the taxpayer – as is explained in paragraph 14 of the Commentary to Article 25 of the OECD Model Tax Convention – should be entitled to set the MAP process in motion. The peer concluded by stating that it would appreciate a further explanation from Indonesia on the likelihood that and/or frequency in which tax assessments are issued in follow-up to the issuing of the letter.

46. In this respect, Indonesia clarified that there may be a misunderstanding at the level of the taxpayer concerning Indonesia's domestic law. It reiterated that the issuing of a letter is just one way of communicating with the taxpayer, for example to obtain information. If the taxpayer would not be able to provide relevant information, or where the relevant information may raise an issue, Indonesia explained that its tax administration may launch an audit. It is only the outcome of this audit, formalised via a tax assessment that may lead to taxation that is not in accordance with the tax treaty and for which the taxpayer may submit a MAP request. In other words, the issuing of a letter would not constitute sufficient ground for a MAP request, since there is no decision yet (or the likelihood thereon) that would cause taxation that is not in accordance with the tax treaty and for which the taxpayer may submit a MAP request. A discussion within the context of the MAP process could in Indonesia's view therefore only be fruitful after the notification of the result of the assessment by the auditor. In any case, Indonesia also expressed that if the peer's competent authority would insist on discussing the case in MAP at the stage where the letter is issued, Indonesia would be willing to do so, regardless how futile the use of resources spent on the case would be.

47. The treaty between Indonesia and this peer contains the equivalent of Article 25(1) of the OECD Model Tax Convention, where it is clearly stated that taxpayers can file a MAP request if there is, or will be, taxation that is not in accordance with the provisions of the treaty. Paragraph 14 of the Commentary to Article 25 of the OECD Model Tax Convention in this respect clarifies that taxpayers can file a MAP request if the taxation that he claims not to be in accordance with the treaty has not been charged against or notified to him. It continues by stating that such taxation is not merely possible, but probable. In that regard, the issuing of an administrative letter by Indonesia's tax administration may not constitute a ground upon which the taxpayer can decide that there is a reasonable risk that a coming action will result for him in taxation not in accordance with the provision of the tax treaty. The fact that Indonesia at that stage does not yet accept the MAP request until there is clarity on whether an adjustment will be made is not against the treaty provision as explained in the Commentary to Article 25 of the OECD Model Tax Convention.

(III) Access to MAP and fiscally transparent entities

48. One peer provided input and reported that in 2018, Indonesia's competent authority indicated that it would not provide treaty benefits or access to MAP with respect to income of fiscally transparent entities that are treated under the peer's domestic legislation as disregarded from its single resident member. The peer specified that the position of Indonesia's competent authority is that a single-member entity does not qualify as a resident under the precise language of the treaty with the peer. In the peer's view, however, the

resident article of its treaty with Indonesia may be interpreted to include a single member of a fiscally transparent entity. The peer further noted that paragraph 3 of the MAP provision of the treaty (being equivalent to Article 25(3), second sentence, of the OECD Model Tax Convention), permits the competent authorities to consult together to resolve difficulties relating to the application of the treaty for the elimination of double taxation in cases not provided for in the treaty. In this respect, the peer encouraged Indonesia's competent authority to enter into an arrangement with the peer's competent authority under that paragraph to resolve this incongruity.

49.   Indonesia provided a response to the input given and mentioned that it recently received a letter from the peer's competent authority seeking a clarification of the issue. It also stressed that Indonesia did not consider the case to be a MAP request, but that it is open to discuss the issue in a competent authority meeting if there is a MAP request on the issue.

50.   The peer reacted and stated that it considered that a taxpayer-specific MAP request is no prerequisite for the competent authorities to engage in discussions to reach a MAP agreement of a general nature, on the basis of the equivalent of Article 25(3), first sentence, of the OECD Model Tax Convention. Such a mutual understanding would in the peer's view help to provide certainty and prevent future disputes on the application of the treaty between the peer and Indonesia, which would benefit both the tax administrations and taxpayers. The peer clarified that the letter that was sent to Indonesia included a request to initiate discussions on status of fiscally transparent entities, with a view to enter into an interpretative MAP agreement. In the peer's view such agreement would be a good use of resources based on the number of inquiries its competent authority received from taxpayers and the attendant uncertainty as regards the eligibility to treaty benefits that is caused by a lack of clarity.

51.   Indonesia reacted and noted that it fully agrees with the peer's view and invites the peer's competent authority to formally send a MAP request on the basis of the equivalent of Article 25(3), first sentence, of the OECD Model Tax Convention.

52.   While the above presented issue is clear, it appears to be more of a general interpretative nature than pertaining to a specific individual case and therefore do not fall in the ambit of analysing whether access to MAP is given in eligible cases.

(IV) Requirement of a subsequent filing of a MAP request in transfer pricing cases

53.   Article 18(4) of Regulation No. 240/PMK.03/2014 stipulates that if a MAP request for a transfer pricing case is submitted at the level of the treaty partner, a filing by the Indonesian associated enterprise is also required, even though the tax treaty requires taxpayers to submit the request in the state of residence.

54.   One peer provided input this issue and reported that since 1 January 2016, 11 attribution/attribution cases were initiated (one in 2016 and ten in 2018), which all related to an adjustment made by Indonesia. The relevant MAP requests were all submitted to the peer's competent authority, for which taxpayers claimed that they were instructed to do so by Indonesia's tax authority, without giving a clear reason. This peer expressed its appreciation if Indonesia could take the necessary steps, including a review of its relevant domestic laws or regulations, to allow taxpayers to present such cases to Indonesia's competent authority with a view of ensuring the availability of and access to MAP in accordance with the Action 14 Minimum Standard.

55.   Another peer stated that it had one pre-2016 attribution/allocation case for which a MAP request was rejected by Indonesia one day before the expiration of three year time limit, because they required that the taxpayer should have submitted a MAP request in Indonesia.

56.   Indonesia responded to the input given by the first peer and mentioned that based on the applicable regulations, it is possible for an Indonesian taxpayer, which is subject to a transfer pricing adjustment, to submit a MAP request in Indonesia. It thereby confirmed that the MAP process would only be initiated once the related taxpayer also filed a MAP request at the level of the treaty partner, such to confirm the occurred double taxation.

57.   The relevant peer provided for a reaction and stated that in its view the practice of Indonesia does not follow the Action 14 Minimum Standard in terms of access to MAP and further that Indonesia should grant access to MAP without having in place such a requirement. It further mentioned that the allowance to file a MAP request in Indonesia is according to Article 7 of Regulation No. 240/PMK.03/2014 only possible for cases whether actions of the treaty partner has led or will lead to taxation that is not in accordance with the provisions of the treaty. In other words, Indonesia does not allow Indonesian resident taxpayers to file a MAP request in Indonesia when the adjustment was taken by its tax administration. The MAP process is in such situation only available to taxpayers when they file a MAP request at the level of the treaty partner, which then opens the process with Indonesia's competent authority. Given this state of play, the peer wondered whether such practice and Indonesia's response is consistent with Article 7 of Regulation No. 240/ PMK.03/2014 and also whether it is compliant with the MAP provision included in Indonesia's tax treaties. The peer therefore expressed that it would highly appreciate if Indonesia could clarify its views on the matter.

58.   Indonesia provided input on the peer's reaction. It stated that in its view a MAP request should be made by the affected taxpayer. If an adjustment is made by Indonesia at the level of the associated enterprise resident in Indonesia, it is thus the associated enterprises that is resident in the peer's state that has to submit a MAP request. To this Indonesia, however, added that it does not imply that the associated enterprise resident in Indonesia cannot submit a MAP request with Indonesia's competent authority.

59.   The tax treaty between the peer and Indonesia contains the equivalent of Article 25(1) of the OECD Model Tax Convention as it read prior to its adoption of the Action 14 final report. Under this provision, taxpayers have the right to submit a MAP request when it considers that there is, or will be, taxation not in accordance with the provisions of the tax treaty due to actions by one or both treaty partners. In that regard, there is no requirement for taxpayers to file a MAP request at the level of one treaty partner, where the adjustment for which the taxpayers submits a MAP request was made by the other treaty partner. Not granting access to MAP in the situation that the taxpayer did not file the request in the first-mentioned state, therefore does not conform with Article 25(1) of the OECD Model Tax Convention.

Article 25(1), second sentence, of the OECD Model Tax Convention

60.   Concerning those treaties that do not contain a filing period for MAP requests, Indonesia reported that there is no limitation for filing of such requests in its domestic legislation and taxpayers are allowed to submit a MAP request without any deadline.

61.   For those treaties that do contain a filing period for MAP request, Article 4(1) of Regulation No. 240/PMK.03/2014 stipulates that a MAP request should be filed within the period as from the date of the first notification of the action that results in taxation that is not in accordance with the provisions of the tax treaty until the end of the time limit specified in the tax treaty. Article 4(2) includes a definition of the term "first notification", which is either the date of the notice of the tax assessment or the date of the withholding tax certificate or other moments specified by the Director General of Taxes, which can be the date of any legal product issued by the tax authorities or the withholding agent.

Anticipated modifications

Multilateral Instrument

Article 25(1), first sentence of the OECD Model Tax Convention

62.   Indonesia signed the Multilateral Instrument. Article 16(4)(a)(i) of that instrument stipulates that Article 16(1), first sentence – containing the equivalent of Article 25(1), first sentence, of the OECD Model Tax Convention as amended by the Action 14 final report and allowing the submission of MAP requests to the competent authority of either contracting state – will apply in place of or in the absence of a provision in tax treaties that is equivalent to Article 25(1), first sentence, of the OECD Model Tax Convention as it read prior to the adoption of the Action 14 final report. However, this shall only apply if both contracting parties to the applicable tax treaty have listed this tax treaty as a covered tax agreement under the Multilateral Instrument and insofar as both notified the depositary, pursuant to Article 16(6)(a), that this treaty contains the equivalent of Article 25(1), first sentence, of the OECD Model Tax Convention as it read prior to the adoption of the Action 14 final report. Article 16(4)(a)(i) will for a tax treaty not take effect if one of the treaty partners has, pursuant to Article 16(5)(a), reserved the right not to apply the first sentence of Article 16(1) of that instrument to all of its covered tax agreements.

63.   Indonesia reserved, pursuant to Article 16(5)(a) of the Multilateral Instrument, the right not to apply the first sentence of Article 16(1) of that instrument to its existing tax treaties, with a view to allow taxpayers to submit a MAP request to the competent authority of either contracting state.[3] In this reservation, Indonesia declared that it would ensure that all of its tax treaties, which are considered covered tax agreements for purposes of the Multilateral Instrument, contain a provision equivalent to Article 25(1), first sentence, of the OECD Model Tax Convention, as it read prior to the adoption of the Action 14 final report. It subsequently declared it would implement a bilateral notification or consultation process for those cases in which its competent authority considers the objection raised by a taxpayer in its MAP request as not being justified. The introduction and application of such process will be further discussed under element B.2.

64.   In view of the above, following the reservation made by Indonesia, those two treaties identified in paragraphs 27 and 29 above that are considered not including the equivalent of Article 25(1), first sentence, of the OECD Model Tax Convention as it read prior to the adoption of the Action 14 final report, will not be modified via the Multilateral Instrument with a view to allow taxpayers to submit a MAP request to the competent authority of either contracting state.

Article 25(1), second sentence of the OECD Model Tax Convention

65.   With respect to the period of filing of a MAP request, Article 16(4)(a)(ii) of the Multilateral Instrument stipulates that Article 16(1), second sentence – containing the equivalent of Article 25(1), second sentence, of the OECD Model Tax Convention – will apply where such period is shorter than three years from the first notification of the action resulting in taxation not in accordance with the provisions of a tax treaty. However, this shall only apply if both contracting parties to the applicable tax treaty have listed this treaty as a covered tax agreement under the Multilateral Instrument and insofar as both notified, pursuant to Article 16(6)(b)(i), the depositary that this treaty does not contain the equivalent of Article 25(1), second sentence, of the OECD Model Tax Convention.

66.   In regard of the 33 tax treaties identified in paragraph 32 above that contain a filing period for MAP requests of less than three years, Indonesia listed 12 treaties as a covered tax agreement under the Multilateral Instrument and for all of them did it make, pursuant to Article 16(6)(b)(i), a notification that they do not contain a provision described in Article 16(4)(a)(ii). Of the 12 relevant treaty partners, two are not a signatory to the Multilateral Instrument, whereas one did not list its treaty with Indonesia as a covered tax agreement under that instrument. All of the remaining nine tax treaties partners also made a notification on the basis of Article 16(6)(b)(i). Therefore, at this stage, nine of the 33 tax treaties identified above will be modified by the Multilateral Instrument upon its entry into force for these treaties to include the equivalent of Article 25(1), second sentence, of the OECD Model Tax Convention.

Bilateral modifications

67.   Indonesia further reported that when the tax treaties that do not contain the equivalent of Article 25(1) of the OECD Model Tax Convention, as it read prior to the adoption of the Action 14 final report, will not be modified by the Multilateral Instrument, it intends to update them via bilateral negotiations with a view to be compliant with element B.1. Indonesia, however, has not put in place a specific plan for such negotiations nor has it taken any actions to that effect. Regardless, Indonesia indicated it will seek to include Article 25(1) of the OECD Model Tax Convention, as it read prior to the adoption of the Action 14 final report, in all of its future tax treaties.

68.   With respect to the first sentence of Article 25(1), Indonesia commented that it is not yet possible to include the equivalent as amended by the Action 14 final report, but it is undergoing the process of amending its law to open the possibility to make the submission of a MAP request to either contracting state.

69.   With respect to the second sentence of Article 25(1), Indonesia reported that for the remaining 24 tax treaties identified above that currently will not be modified, it will modify its notifications under Article 16(6)(d)(i) of the Multilateral Instrument to include these treaties. If done so, the expected impact hereof would be that eight more treaties will be modified by that instrument, bringing the total to 17 treaties and with 16 treaties left for which bilateral negotiations are necessary.

Other anticipated modifications

70.   For those treaties that do not contain a filing period for MAP requests, although these treaties are not contrary to the Action 14 Minimum Standard, Indonesia reported that it plans to change Regulation 240/PMK.03/2014 to set a deadline for filing of MAP requests of no less than three years from the first notification of the action resulting in taxation not in accordance with the provisions of the tax treaty. Indonesia specified that this change is currently in the legislative process and is expected to be published in 2019.

71.   In addition, Indonesia also reported that it plans to clarify in the update to the Minister of Finance Regulation No. 240/PMK.03/2014 that taxpayers can file a MAP request even when domestic court has finalised the hearing process and that access to MAP will be granted in such cases.

Peer input

72.   Most of the peers that provided input indicated that their treaty with Indonesia meets the requirements under element B.1, which is nearly in conformity with the analysis of this section. One of these peers is party to a treaty that does not contain the equivalent of Article 25(1), first and sentence, of the OECD Model Tax Convention. Concerning the other treaties that do not contain this equivalent, the relevant peers did not provide input.

Conclusion

	Areas for improvement	Recommendations
[B.1]	Two out of 72 tax treaties do not contain a provision that is equivalent to Article 25(1), first sentence, of the OECD Model Tax Convention and the timeline to file a MAP request is shorter than three years from the first notification of the action resulting in taxation not in accordance with the provision of the tax treaty. Of these two treaties, one is expected to be modified by the Multilateral Instrument to include Article 25(1), second sentence.	Indonesia should as quickly as possible ratify the Multilateral Instrument to incorporate the equivalent to Article 25(1), second sentence, of the OECD Model Tax Convention in the treaty that currently does not contain such equivalent and that will be modified by the Multilateral Instrument upon its entry into force for the treaties concerned. Since this treaty will not be modified by the Multilateral Instrument as regards the first sentence of Article 25(1), Indonesia should also follow its stated intention to request the inclusion of the required provision via bilateral negotiations. This concerns a provision that is equivalent to Article 25(1), first sentence of the OECD Model Tax Convention either: a. as amended in the Action 14 final report; or b. as it read prior to the adoption of Action 14 final report, thereby including the full sentence of such provision. Furthermore, for the other treaty that will not be modified by the Multilateral Instrument to incorporate the equivalent to Article 25(1), first and second sentence, of the OECD Model Tax Convention, Indonesia should also follow its stated intention to request the inclusion of the required provision via bilateral negotiations, which also regards one of the options identified above. To this end, Indonesia should put a plan in place on how it envisages updating this treaty to include the required provision.
	31 out of 72 tax treaties does not contain the equivalent of Article 25(1), second sentence, of the OECD Model Tax Convention, as the timeline to file a MAP request is shorter than three years from the first notification of the action resulting in taxation not in accordance with the provision of the tax treaty. With respect to these 31 treaties • Eight are expected to be modified by the Multilateral Instrument to include the required provision. • Eight are expected to be modified by the Multilateral Instrument to include the required provision, once the notifications under that instrument are modified.	Indonesia should as quickly as possible follow its stated intention and modify its notifications under the Multilateral Instrument and subsequently ratify that instrument to incorporate the equivalent to Article 25(1), second sentence, of the OECD Model Tax Convention in those 116 treaties that currently do not contain such equivalent and that will be modified by the Multilateral Instrument upon its entry into force for the treaties concerned. For the remaining 15 treaties that currently do not contain such equivalent and that will not be modified by the Multilateral Instrument to include the equivalent to Article 25(1), first sentence, of the OECD Model Tax Convention, Indonesia should follow its stated intention to request the inclusion of the required provision. To this end, Indonesia should put a plan in place on how it envisages updating these 15 treaties to include the required provision.

	Areas for improvement	Recommendations
		In addition, Indonesia should maintain its stated intention to include Article 25(1) of the OECD Model Tax Convention in all future tax treaties.
[B.1]	Access to MAP will be denied in certain cases, even when the requirements for initiating a MAP case under the treaty provision that is equivalent to Article 25(1) of the OECD Model Tax Convention are met. This in particular concerns: • cases where domestic courts have already rendered a decision on the issue for which MAP request is submitted, but also where such court decision regards the same taxpayer but is not related to an issue for which a MAP request was submitted • the requirement of filing a MAP request at the level of the treaty partner for adjustments made by Indonesia	Indonesia should ensure that access to MAP is given in all eligible cases where the requirements under Article 25(1) of the OECD Model Tax convention as incorporated in Indonesia's tax treaties have been met. In particular, Indonesia should not limit such access in cases: • where domestic courts have rendered a decision relating, or not relating, to cases for which a MAP request was submitted • where the taxpayer did not file a MAP request at the level of the treaty partner for adjustments made by Indonesia.

[B.2] Allow submission of MAP requests to the competent authority of either treaty partner, or, alternatively, introduce a bilateral consultation or notification process

> Jurisdictions should ensure that either (i) their tax treaties contain a provision which provides that the taxpayer can make a request for MAP assistance to the competent authority of either Contracting Party, or (ii) where the treaty does not permit a MAP request to be made to either Contracting Party and the competent authority who received the MAP request from the taxpayer does not consider the taxpayer's objection to be justified, the competent authority should implement a bilateral consultation or notification process which allows the other competent authority to provide its views on the case (such consultation shall not be interpreted as consultation as to how to resolve the case).

73.   In order to ensure that all competent authorities concerned are aware of MAP requests submitted, for a proper consideration of the request by them and to ensure that taxpayers have effective access to MAP in eligible cases, it is essential that all tax treaties contain a provision that either allows taxpayers to submit a MAP request to the competent authority:

  i.   of either treaty partner; or, in the absence of such provision,

  ii. where it is a resident, or to the competent authority of the state of which they are a national if their cases come under the non-discrimination article. In such cases, jurisdictions should have in place a bilateral consultation or notification process where a competent authority considers the objection raised by the taxpayer in a MAP request as being not justified.

Domestic bilateral consultation or notification process in place

74.   As discussed under element B.1, none of Indonesia's 72 treaties currently contains a provision equivalent to Article 25(1), first sentence, of the OECD Model Tax Convention as changed by the Action 14 final report, allowing taxpayers to submit a MAP request to the competent authority of either treaty partner. As previously discussed under element B.1, none of these tax treaties will, following Indonesia's reservation according to Article 16(5)(a) of the Multilateral Instrument, be modified by that instrument to allow taxpayers to submit a MAP request to the competent authority of either contracting state.

75.   Indonesia reported that internal regulations for staff in charge of MAP cases dictates that any incoming MAP request or notification of such a request by the treaty partner should be submitted to a specific email address and also be submitted via an official letter. In Indonesia's view this process could effectively work to accommodate the bilateral consultation process to be applied when its competent authority considers the objection raised in a MAP request as not being justified and to allow the other competent authority concerned to provide its views on the case. In this respect, Indonesia further clarified that internal regulations define in what circumstances staff in charge of a MAP may arrive at such a conclusion and further contains instructions for such staff to consult with the treaty partner before closing the case.[4]

76.   Further to the above, Article 9(2) of Regulation No. 240/PMK.03/2014 stipulates that if a MAP request is not accepted into the process, the competent authority will inform the taxpayer hereof, thereby specifying the reasons that lead to this decision.

Practical application

77.   Indonesia reported that since 1 January 2016 its competent authority has for none of the MAP requests it received decided that the objection raised by taxpayers in such request was not justified. The 2016-18 MAP statistics submitted by Indonesia also show that none of its MAP cases was closed with the outcome "objection not justified". [to be confirmed with the 2018 MAP statistics]

78.   All peers that provided input indicated not being aware of any cases for which Indonesia's competent authority denied access to MAP since 1 January 2016. They also reported not having been consulted/notified of a case where Indonesia's competent authority considered the objection raised in a MAP request as not justified since that date, which can be clarified by the fact that no such instances have occurred in Indonesia during this period.

Anticipated modifications

79.   Indonesia indicated that it does not anticipate any modifications in relation to element B.2.

Conclusion

	Areas for improvement	Recommendations
[B.2]	Indonesia has a documented process in place to consult the other competent authority in cases where the objection raised in the MAP request was considered as being not justified. However, it was not possible to assess whether the consultation or notification process is applied in practice because during the Review period no such cases have occurred.	

[B.3] Provide access to MAP in transfer pricing cases

> Jurisdictions should provide access to MAP in transfer pricing cases.

80.   Where two or more tax administrations take different positions on what constitutes arm's length conditions for specific transactions between associated enterprises, economic double taxation may occur. Not granting access to MAP with respect to a treaty partner's transfer pricing adjustment, with a view to eliminating the economic double taxation that may arise from such adjustment, will likely frustrate the main objective of tax treaties. Jurisdictions should thus provide access to MAP in transfer pricing cases.

Legal and administrative framework

81.   Out of Indonesia's 72 tax treaties, 48 contain a provision that is equivalent to Article 9(2) of the OECD Model Tax Convention requiring their state to make a correlative adjustment in case a transfer pricing adjustment is imposed by the treaty partner. Furthermore, 21 treaties do not contain such equivalent.

82.   The remaining four treaties can be categorised as follows:

- Two contain a provision that is based on Article 9(2) of the OECD Model Tax Convention, but deviate from it as corresponding adjustments can only be granted on the basis of a mutual agreement between the competent authorities.

- One contains a provision that is based on Article 9(2) of the OECD Model Tax Convention, but the granting of a corresponding adjustment is only optional as the word "shall" is used instead of "may".

- One contains a provision that is based on Article 9(2) of the OECD Model Tax Convention, but contains does not incorporate the last sentence of that provision.

83.   In view of these four treaties, Indonesia specified that it will facilitate corresponding adjustments, irrespective of whether the treaty concerns the word "may" instead of "shall". In Indonesia's view the word "may" cannot be interpreted to make the adjustment only optional without a valid and strong reason.

84.   Access to MAP should be provided in transfer pricing cases regardless of whether the equivalent of Article 9(2) is contained in Indonesia's tax treaties and irrespective of whether its domestic legislation enables the granting of corresponding adjustments. In accordance with element B.3, as translated from the Action 14 Minimum Standard, Indonesia indicated that it will always provide access to MAP for transfer pricing cases and is willing to make corresponding adjustments, regardless of whether the equivalent of Article 9(2) of the OECD Model Tax Convention is contained in its tax treaties. In that regard, Indonesia mentioned that there has been MAP cases under a treaty that does not contain such equivalent and where access to MAP was granted.

85.   In view of the above, Article 7(1) of the Minister of Finance Regulation No. 240/PMK.03/2014 includes examples of cases for which taxpayers can submit a MAP requests, which include cases concerning transfer pricing adjustments. Furthermore, Article 17(1) of this regulates also includes examples of such cases, which regards MAP cases initiated at the level of the treaty partner. These example also concern transfer pricing adjustments and corresponding adjustments, and that it will grant access to MAP for such cases.

Application of legal and administrative framework in practice

86.   Indonesia reported that since 1 January 2016, it has not denied access to MAP on the basis that the case concerned a transfer pricing case.

87.   All peers that provided input indicated that they are not being aware of a denial of access to MAP by Indonesia since 1 January 2016 on the basis that the case concerned was a transfer pricing case.

Anticipated modifications

88.   Indonesia reported that it is in favour of including Article 9(2) of the OECD Model Tax Convention in its tax treaties where possible and that it will seek to include this provision in all of its future tax treaties. In that regard, Indonesia signed the Multilateral

Instrument. Article 17(2) of that instrument stipulates that Article 17(1) – containing the equivalent of Article 9(2) of the OECD Model Tax Convention – will apply in place of or in the absence of a provision in tax treaties that is equivalent to Article 9(2) of the OECD Model Tax Convention. However, this shall only apply if both contracting parties to the applicable tax treaty have listed this treaty as a covered tax agreement under the Multilateral Instrument. Article 17(2) of the Multilateral Instrument does not take effect for a tax treaty if one or both of the treaty partners have, pursuant to Article 17(3), reserved the right not to apply Article 17(2) for those tax treaties that already contain the equivalent of Article 9(2) of the OECD Model Tax Convention, or not to apply Article 17(2) in the absence of such equivalent under the condition that: (i) it shall make appropriate corresponding adjustments or (ii) its competent authority shall endeavour to resolve the case under mutual agreement procedure of the applicable tax treaty. Where neither treaty partner has made such a reservation, Article 17(4) of the Multilateral Instrument stipulates that both have to notify the depositary whether the applicable treaty already contains a provision equivalent to Article 9(2) of the OECD Model Tax Convention. Where such a notification is made by both of them, the Multilateral Instrument will modify this treaty to replace that provision. If neither or only one treaty partner made this notification, Article 17(1) of the Multilateral Instrument will supersede this treaty only to the extent that the provision contained in that treaty relating to the granting of corresponding adjustments is incompatible with Article 17(1) (containing the equivalent of Article 9(2) of the OECD Model Tax Convention).

89.   Indonesia has, pursuant to Article 17(3), reserved the right not to apply Article 17(2) of the Multilateral Instrument on the basis that in the absence of a provision referred to in Article 17(2) in its covered tax agreement: (i) it shall make the appropriate adjustment referred to in Article 17(1); or (ii) its competent authority shall endeavour to resolve the case under the provisions of a covered tax agreement relating to mutual agreement procedure. In view of the reservation made by Indonesia, the 25 treaties identified in paragraphs 80 and 81 above that are considered not to contain a provision that is equivalent to Article 9(2) of the OECD Model Tax Convention will not be modified via the Multilateral Instrument to include such provision.

90.   Indonesia reported that it is in favour of including Article 9(2) of the OECD Model Tax Convention in its tax treaties where possible and that it will seek to include it in all of . its future tax treaties.

Conclusion

	Areas for improvement	Recommendations
[B.3]	-	As Indonesia has thus far granted access to MAP in eligible transfer pricing cases, it should continue granting access for these cases.

[B.4]   Provide access to MAP in relation to the application of anti-abuse provisions

> Jurisdictions should provide access to MAP in cases in which there is a disagreement between the taxpayer and the tax authorities making the adjustment as to whether the conditions for the application of a treaty anti-abuse provision have been met or as to whether the application of a domestic law anti-abuse provision is in conflict with the provisions of a treaty.

91.   There is no general rule denying access to MAP in cases of perceived abuse. In order to protect taxpayers from arbitrary application of anti-abuse provisions in tax treaties and in

order to ensure that competent authorities have a common understanding on such application, it is important that taxpayers have access to MAP if they consider the interpretation and/or application of a treaty anti-abuse provision as being incorrect. Subsequently, to avoid cases in which the application of domestic anti-abuse legislation is in conflict with the provisions of a tax treaty, it is also important that taxpayers have access to MAP in such cases.

Legal and administrative framework

92.   None of Indonesia's 72 tax treaties allow competent authorities to restrict access to MAP for cases where a treaty anti-abuse provision applies or where there is a disagreement between the taxpayer and the tax authorities as to whether the application of a domestic law anti-abuse provision is in conflict with the provisions of a tax treaty. In addition, also the domestic law and/or administrative processes of Indonesia do not include a provision allowing its competent authority to limit access to MAP for cases in which there is a disagreement between the taxpayer and the tax authorities as to whether the conditions for the application of a domestic law anti-abuse provision is in conflict with the provisions of a tax treaty.

93.   Indonesia reported that it will provide access to MAP in cases concerning the application of a treaty anti-abuse provision or for cases concerning the question whether the application of the domestic anti-abuse provision comes into conflict with the provision of a tax treaty. In this regard, the Minister of Finance Regulation No. 240/PMK.03/2014 does not contain information whether access to MAP is available for such cases.

Practical application

94.   Indonesia reported that since 1 January 2016 Indonesia's competent authority has received MAP requests for cases in which there was a disagreement between the taxpayer and the tax authorities as to whether the conditions for the application of a treaty anti-abuse provision have been met, or as to whether the application of a domestic law anti-abuse provision is in conflict with the provisions of a tax treaty, and it has not denied access to MAP for these cases.

95.   All peers that provided input indicated not being aware of cases that have been denied access to MAP in Indonesia since 1 January 2016 in relation to the application of treaty and/or domestic anti-abuse provisions.

Anticipated modifications

96.   Indonesia indicated that it does not anticipate any modifications in relation to element B.4.

Conclusion

	Areas for improvement	Recommendations
[B.4]	-	As Indonesia has thus far granted access to MAP in eligible cases concerning whether the conditions for the application of a treaty anti-abuse provision have been met or whether the application of a domestic law anti-abuse provision is in conflict with the provisions of a treaty, it should continue granting access for these cases.

[B.5] Provide access to MAP in cases of audit settlements

> Jurisdictions should not deny access to MAP in cases where there is an audit settlement between tax authorities and taxpayers. If jurisdictions have an administrative or statutory dispute settlement/resolution process independent from the audit and examination functions and that can only be accessed through a request by the taxpayer, jurisdictions may limit access to the MAP with respect to the matters resolved through that process.

97.   An audit settlement procedure can be valuable to taxpayers by providing certainty on their tax position. Nevertheless, as double taxation may not be fully eliminated by agreeing on such settlements, taxpayers should have access to the MAP in such cases, unless they were already resolved via an administrative or statutory disputes settlement/resolution process that functions independently from the audit and examination function and which is only accessible through a request by taxpayers.

Legal and administrative framework

Audit settlements

98.   Indonesia reported that under its domestic law no process is available allowing taxpayers and the tax administration to enter into a settlement during the course of or after ending of an audit.

Administrative or statutory dispute settlement/resolution process

99.   Indonesia reported that it has no administrative or statutory dispute settlement/ resolution process in place, which is independent from the audit and examination functions and can only be accessed through a request by the taxpayer.

Practical application

100.   In view of the fact that it is in Indonesia not possible that the taxpayer and the tax administration enter into audit settlements, Indonesia reported that since 1 January 2016 it has not denied access to MAP for cases where the issue presented by the taxpayer in a MAP request has already been resolved through an audit settlement between the taxpayer and the tax administration.

101.   All peers that provided input indicated not being aware of a denial of access to MAP in Indonesia since 1 January 2016 in cases where there was an audit settlement between the taxpayer and the tax administration, which can be clarified by the fact that no such process is in place in Indonesia.

Anticipated modifications

102.   Indonesia indicated that it does not anticipate any modifications in relation to element B.5.

Conclusion

	Areas for improvement	Recommendations
[B.5]	-	-

[B.6]   Provide access to MAP if required information is submitted

> Jurisdictions should not limit access to MAP based on the argument that insufficient information was provided if the taxpayer has provided the required information based on the rules, guidelines and procedures made available to taxpayers on access to and the use of MAP.

103.   To resolve cases where there is taxation not in accordance with the provisions of the tax treaty, it is important that competent authorities do not limit access to MAP when taxpayers have complied with the information and documentation requirements as provided in the jurisdiction's guidance relating hereto. Access to MAP will be facilitated when such required information and documentation is made publicly available.

Legal framework on access to MAP and information to be submitted

104.   The information and documentation Indonesia requires taxpayers to include in a request for MAP assistance are discussed under element B.8.

105.   Indonesia reported that where a taxpayer has not provided all required information in its MAP request, Indonesia's competent authority will request the taxpayer to submit the missing/additional information and/or documentation as set forth in Article 8(2) and Article 13(2) of the Minister of Finance Regulation No. 240/PMK.03/2014. This provision stipulates that Indonesia's competent authority can request a further explanation of the taxpayer that filed the MAP request, which includes requesting supporting documents or other necessary information. If such additional information is requested, taxpayers should provide this information within the time frame that is set forth in the request. When taxpayers do not comply with this request for information, Indonesia reported it will not limit access to MAP, but will proceed with the MAP case based on available information. However, in Article 26(1)(a) of Regulation No. 240/PMK.03/2014 it is stipulated that the non-submission of all required information is a ground to end proceedings. Indonesia clarified that in practice it has never ended the MAP process because taxpayers did not file the required information and that the Article is only intended to push the taxpayer to fulfil the requirements of providing information in a timely manner.

Practical application

106.   Indonesia reported that it provided access to MAP in all cases where taxpayers have complied with the information or documentation requirements as set out in its MAP guidance. It further reported that since 1 January 2016 it has not denied access to MAP for cases where the taxpayer had not provided the required information or documentation.

107.   All peers that provided input indicated not being aware of a limitation of access to MAP by Indonesia since 1 January 2016 in situations where taxpayers complied with information and documentation requirements.

Anticipated modifications

108.   Indonesia indicated that it does not anticipate any modifications in relation to element B.6.

Conclusion

	Areas for improvement	Recommendations
[B.6]	-	As Indonesia has thus far not limited access to MAP in eligible cases when taxpayers have complied with Indonesia's information and documentation requirements for MAP requests, it should continue this practice.

[B.7] Include Article 25(3), second sentence, of the OECD Model Tax Convention in tax treaties

Jurisdictions should ensure that their tax treaties contain a provision under which competent authorities may consult together for the elimination of double taxation in cases not provided for in their tax treaties.

109. For ensuring that tax treaties operate effectively and in order for competent authorities to be able to respond quickly to unanticipated situations, it is useful that tax treaties include the second sentence of Article 25(3) of the OECD Model Tax Convention, enabling them to consult together for the elimination of double taxation in cases not provided for by these treaties.

Current situation of Indonesia's tax treaties

110. Out of Indonesia's 72 tax treaties, 66 contain a provision equivalent to Article 25(3), second sentence, of the OECD Model Tax Convention allowing their competent authorities to consult together for the elimination of double taxation in cases not provided for in their tax treaties. The remaining six treaties do not contain a provision that based on, or equivalent to, Article 25(3), second sentence, of the OECD Model Tax Convention.

Anticipated modifications

Multilateral Instrument

111. Indonesia signed the Multilateral Instrument. Article 16(4)(c)(ii) of that instrument stipulates that Article 16(3), second sentence – containing the equivalent of Article 25(3), second sentence, of the OECD Model Tax Convention – will apply in the absence of a provision in tax treaties that is equivalent to Article 25(3), second sentence, of the OECD Model Tax Convention. In other words, in the absence of this equivalent, Article 16(4)(c)(ii) of the Multilateral Instrument will modify the applicable tax treaty to include such equivalent. However, this shall only apply if both contracting parties to the applicable tax treaty have listed this treaty as a covered tax agreement under the Multilateral Instrument and insofar as both notified, pursuant to Article 16(6)(d)(ii), the depositary that this treaty does not contain the equivalent of Article 25(3), second sentence, of the OECD Model Tax Convention.

112. In regard of the six tax treaties identified above that are considered not to contain the equivalent of Article 25(3), second sentence, of the OECD Model Tax Convention, Indonesia listed five of them as a covered tax agreement under the Multilateral Instrument and for two of them did it make, pursuant to Article 16(6)(d)(ii), a notification that they do not contain a provision described in Article 16(4)(c)(ii). The relevant two treaty partners, being a signatory to the Multilateral Instrument, listed their treaty with Indonesia as a covered tax agreement and also made such notification. Therefore, at this stage, two of the

six tax treaties identified above will be modified by the Multilateral Instrument upon its entry into force for these treaties to include the equivalent of Article 25(3), second sentence, of the OECD Model Tax Convention.

Bilateral modifications

113.   Indonesia reported that for the four tax treaties that do not contain the equivalent of Article 25(3), second sentence, of the OECD Model Tax Convention and that will not be modified by the Multilateral Instrument, it will modify its notifications under Article 16(6)(d)(ii) of the Multilateral Instrument to include these treaties. If done so, the expected impact hereof would be that all of these treaties will be modified by that instrument, following which there would not be a need for bilateral modifications. Regardless, Indonesia reported it will seek to include Article 25(3), second sentence, of the OECD Model Tax Convention in all of its future tax treaties.

Peer input

114.   Nearly all of peers that provided input indicated that their treaty with Indonesia meets the requirements under element B.7, which conforms with the analysis of this section. For the six treaties identified that do not contain the equivalent of Article 25(3), second sentence, of the OECD Model Tax Convention, two of the relevant peers provided input and confirmed the absence of such equivalent in their treaties.

Conclusion

	Areas for improvement	Recommendations
[B.7]	Six out of 72 tax treaties do not contain a provision that is equivalent to Article 25(3), second sentence, of the OECD Model Tax Convention. With respect to these six treaties: • Two are expected to be modified by the Multilateral Instrument to include the required provision. • Four are expected to be modified by the Multilateral Instrument to include the required provision, once the notifications under that instrument are modified.	Indonesia should as quickly as possible follow its stated intention and modify its notifications under the Multilateral Instrument and subsequently ratify that instrument to incorporate the equivalent to Article 25(3), second sentence, of the OECD Model Tax Convention in those six treaties that currently do not contain such equivalent and that will be modified by the Multilateral Instrument upon its entry into force for the treaties concerned. In addition, Indonesia should maintain its stated intention to include the required provision in all future tax treaties.

[B.8]   Publish clear and comprehensive MAP guidance

Jurisdictions should publish clear rules, guidelines and procedures on access to and use of the MAP and include the specific information and documentation that should be submitted in a taxpayer's request for MAP assistance.

115.   Information on a jurisdiction's MAP regime facilitates the timely initiation and resolution of MAP cases. Clear rules, guidelines and procedures on access to and use of the MAP are essential for making taxpayers and other stakeholders aware of how a jurisdiction's MAP regime functions. In addition, to ensure that a MAP request is received and will be reviewed by the competent authority in a timely manner, it is important that a jurisdiction's MAP guidance clearly and comprehensively explains how a taxpayer can make a MAP request and what information and documentation should be included in such request.

Indonesia's MAP guidance

116.   Indonesia has issued several rules, guidelines and procedures in relation its MAP programme. The basis hereof is the Government Regulation No. 74/2011, which in Articles 57 and 58 include the legal basis of Indonesia's MAP programme. Furthermore, Article 59 stipulates that further provisions regarding the mutual agreement procedure shall be stipulated by means of a regulation by the Minister of Finance. In follow up hereto, Indonesia issued on 22 December 2014 the Minister of Finance Regulation No. 240/ PMK.03/2014 on the implementation of guidelines on the mutual agreement procedure, which includes detailed information on its MAP programme. This regulation is available at:

https://www.pajak.go.id/sites/default/files/2019-03/PMK-240-2014%20%28EN%29.pdf

117.   This regulation consists of eight chapters, which are: (i) general provisions, (ii) scope of the MAP process, eligibility of cases and formal requirements for MAP requests, (iii) the MAP process if a MAP request is submitted by an Indonesian taxpayer, (iv) the MAP process if a MAP is initiated at the own initiative of the Director General of Taxes, (v) MAP process if a MAP request is at the level of the treaty partner, (vi) the organisation of the competent authority function in Indonesia, (vii) the process for implementing MAP agreements and (viii) miscellaneous provisions. In more detail, this MAP guidance contains information on:

    a.   the manner in which the taxpayer should submit its MAP request

    b.   the specific information and documentation that should be included in a MAP request (see also below)

    c.   how the MAP functions in terms of timing and the role of the competent authorities

    d.   relationship with domestic available remedies

    e.   access to MAP in transfer pricing cases

    f.   suspension of tax collection during the period a MAP case is pending

    g.   implementation of MAP agreements.

118.   Further to the above, Indonesia also established a dedicated webpage containing information on its APA and MAP programme. The information contained on this website describes in its practical sense how Indonesia's MAP programme operates in practice and reproduces the content of the regulation. It is specifically stated that the information should be read in conjunction with Regulation No. 240/PMK.03.2014. The following subjects are covered: (i) definition of a MAP, (ii) the aim of the MAP, (iii) eligibility of cases for MAP, (iv) outline of the MAP process, (v) applicable time limits for the submission of MAP request and information to be included in such a request, (vi) process for implementing MAP agreements, (vii) MAP statistics and (viii) contact details of the competent authority. This webpage is available at:

www.pajak.go.id/apa-map

119.   The above-described MAP guidance of Indonesia, and the information contained on the website, includes detailed information on the availability and the use of MAP and how its competent authority conducts the procedure in practice. This guidance partially includes part of the information that the FTA MAP Forum agreed should be included in a jurisdiction's MAP guidance.[5] While the manner and form in which the taxpayer should submit its MAP request is described, contact information of the competent authority or the office in charge of MAP cases is not contained. In that regard, the MAP guidance also no longer refers to the correct directorate in its definition of the competent authority.

120. Furthermore, although the information included in Indonesia's MAP guidance is detailed and comprehensive, various subjects are not specifically discussed in Indonesia's MAP guidance. This concerns information on:

- whether MAP is available in cases of: (i) the application of anti-abuse provisions, (ii) multilateral disputes and (iii) bona fide foreign-initiated self-adjustments
- whether taxpayers can request for the multi-year resolution of recurring issues through MAP
- confidentiality of information throughout the MAP process
- the consideration of interest and penalties in the MAP.

Information and documentation to be included in a MAP request

121. To facilitate the review of a MAP request by competent authorities and to have more consistency in the required content of MAP requests, the FTA MAP Forum agreed on guidance that jurisdictions could use in their domestic guidance on what information and documentation taxpayers need to include in request for MAP assistance.[6] This agreed guidance is shown below. Indonesia's MAP guidance enumerating in Article 7 which items must be included in a request for MAP assistance (if available) are checked in the following list:[7]

- ☑ identity of the taxpayer(s) covered in the MAP request
- ☑ the basis for the request
- ☑ facts of the case
- ☑ analysis of the issue(s) requested to be resolved via MAP
- ☐ whether the MAP request was also submitted to the competent authority of the other treaty partner
- ☐ whether the MAP request was also submitted to another authority under another instrument that provides for a mechanism to resolve treaty-related disputes
- ☐ whether the issue(s) involved were dealt with previously
- ☐ a statement confirming that all information and documentation provided in the MAP request is accurate and that the taxpayer will assist the competent authority in its resolution of the issue(s) presented in the MAP request by furnishing any other information or documentation required by the competent authority in a timely manner.

122. Further to the above, Indonesia's MAP guidance in Article 7(3) specifies that the MAP request should be filed in the Indonesian language.

Anticipated modifications

123. Indonesia reported that it is finalising a legislative process to amend the Minister of Finance Regulation No. 240/PMK.03/2014, which is expected to be published in 2019. The amendments will clarify that:

- access to MAP is available in a broad range of cases, which *inter alia* concerns that MAP requests can be submitted for corresponding adjustment
- taxpayers can submit a MAP request within a period of a maximum three years from the first notification of the action that result in or will result in the imposition

of taxation not in accordance with tax treaty, when the tax treaty does not contain a filing period for MAP requests

- a targeted period of a maximum of 24 months is set for the resolution of MAP cases

- establishing the timeframe for the implementation of MAP agreements

- there will be standardised forms and documents for a MAP request, withdrawal, and the decree for the implementation of MAP agreements.

Conclusion

	Areas for improvement	Recommendations
[B.8]	-	Although not required by the Action 14 Minimum Standard, in order to further improve the level of details of its MAP guidance Indonesia could consider including information on: • whether MAP is available in cases of: (i) the application of anti-abuse provisions, (ii) multilateral disputes and (iii) bona fide foreign-initiated self-adjustments • whether taxpayers can request for the multi-year resolution of recurring issues through MAP • the consideration of interest and penalties in the MAP. Furthermore, as was suggested by a peer (reflected under element B.1), Indonesia could also consider including information how the effects of a judicial decision affects the MAP process, since taxpayers and treaty partners may not fully understand such effects.

[B.9] Make MAP guidance available and easily accessible and publish MAP profile

> Jurisdictions should take appropriate measures to make rules, guidelines and procedures on access to and use of the MAP available and easily accessible to the public and should publish their jurisdiction MAP profiles on a shared public platform pursuant to the agreed template.

124. The public availability and accessibility of a jurisdiction's MAP guidance increases public awareness on access to and the use of the MAP in that jurisdiction. Publishing MAP profiles on a shared public platform further promotes the transparency and dissemination of the MAP programme.[8]

Rules, guidelines and procedures on access to and use of the MAP

125. Indonesia's MAP guidance (Minister of Finance Regulation No. 240/PMK.03/2014) is published and available at:

https://www.pajak.go.id/sites/default/files/2019-03/PMK-240-2014%20%28EN%29.pdf

126. As regards its accessibility, Indonesia's MAP guidance can easily be found on the webpage titled with "APA MAP" of the website of Indonesia's tax administration. It can also be easily found via the website:

www.pajak.go.id/apa-map

MAP profile

127. Indonesia's MAP profile is published on the website of the OECD. This MAP profile is almost complete and often with detailed information. This profile includes external links that provide extra information and guidance where appropriate. Indonesia's MAP, however, is not entirely clear, as its position on MAP arbitration is not clarified, which will be further discussed under element C.6.

Anticipated modifications

128. Indonesia indicated that it does not anticipate any modifications in relation to element B.9.

Conclusion

	Areas for improvement	**Recommendations**
[B.9]	-	As it has thus far made its MAP guidance available and easily accessible and published its MAP profile, Indonesia should ensure that its future updates to the MAP guidance continue to be publicly available and easily accessible and that its MAP profile published on the shared public platform is updated if needed.

[B.10] Clarify in MAP guidance that audit settlements do not preclude access to MAP

> Jurisdictions should clarify in their MAP guidance that audit settlements between tax authorities and taxpayers do not preclude access to MAP. If jurisdictions have an administrative or statutory dispute settlement/resolution process independent from the audit and examination functions and that can only be accessed through a request by the taxpayer, and jurisdictions limit access to the MAP with respect to the matters resolved through that process, jurisdictions should notify their treaty partners of such administrative or statutory processes and should expressly address the effects of those processes with respect to the MAP in their public guidance on such processes and in their public MAP programme guidance.

129. As explained under element B.5, an audit settlement can be valuable to taxpayers by providing certainty to them on their tax position. Nevertheless, as double taxation may not be fully eliminated by agreeing with such settlements, it is important that a jurisdiction's MAP guidance clarifies that in case of audit settlement taxpayers have access to the MAP. In addition, for providing clarity on the relationship between administrative or statutory dispute settlement or resolution processes and the MAP (if any), it is critical that both the public guidance on such processes and the public MAP programme guidance address the effects of those processes, if any. Finally, as the MAP represents a collaborative approach between treaty partners, it is helpful that treaty partners are notified of each other's MAP programme and limitations thereto, particularly in relation to the previously mentioned processes.

MAP and audit settlements in the MAP guidance

130. As previously discussed under B.5, under Indonesia's domestic law it is not possible that taxpayers and the tax administration enter into audit settlements. In that regard, there is no need for Indonesia to address in its MAP guidance whether taxpayers can have access to MAP in such circumstances.

131.   Peers raised no issues with respect to the availability of audit settlements and the inclusion of information hereon in Indonesia's MAP guidance.

MAP and other administrative or statutory dispute settlement/resolution processes in available guidance

132.   As previously mentioned under element B.5, Indonesia does not have an administrative or statutory dispute settlement/resolution process in place that is independent from the audit and examination functions and can only be accessed through a request by the taxpayer and that may affect access to MAP. In this regard, there is no need to address the effects of such process with respect to MAP in Indonesia's MAP guidance.

133.   All peers that provided input indicated not being aware of the existence of an administrative or statutory dispute settlement/resolution process that may limit access to MAP in Indonesia, which can be clarified by the fact that such process is not in place in Indonesia.

Notification of treaty partners of existing administrative or statutory dispute settlement/resolution processes

134.   As Indonesia does not have an internal administrative or statutory dispute settlement/resolution process in Indonesia relevant to MAP in place, there is no need for Indonesia to notify its treaty partners of such process.

Anticipated modifications

135.   Indonesia indicated that it does not anticipate any modifications in relation to element B.10.

Conclusion

	Areas for improvement	Recommendations
[B.10]	-	-

Notes

1.   Indonesia's website containing information on MAP and APAs also explains the relationship between MAP and domestic remedies, which outline is similar as the content of the regulations. Available at: www.pajak.go.id/apa-map.

2.   See also www.pajak.go.id/apa-map, paragraph 6.

3.   This reservation on Article 16 – Mutual Agreement Procedure reads: "Pursuant to Article 16(5) (a) of the Convention, Indonesia reserves the right for the first sentence of Article 16(1) not to apply to its Covered Tax Agreements on the basis that it intends to meet the minimum standard for improving dispute resolution under the OECD/G20 BEPS Package by ensuring that under each of its Covered Tax Agreements (other than a Covered Tax Agreement that permits a person to present a case to the competent authority of either Contracting Jurisdiction), where a person

considers that the actions of one or both of the Contracting Jurisdictions result or will result for that person in taxation not in accordance with the provisions of the Covered Tax Agreement, irrespective of the remedies provided by the domestic law of those Contracting Jurisdictions, that person may present the case to the competent authority of the Contracting Jurisdiction of which the person is a resident or, if the case presented by that person comes under a provision of a Covered Tax Agreement relating to non-discrimination based on nationality, to that of the Contracting Jurisdiction of which that person is a national; and the competent authority of that Contracting Jurisdiction will implement a bilateral notification or consultation process with the competent authority of the other Contracting Jurisdiction for cases in which the competent authority to which the mutual agreement procedure case was presented does not consider the taxpayer's objection to be justified." An overview of Indonesia's positions on the Multilateral Instrument is available at: www.oecd.org/tax/treaties/beps-mli-position-indonesia.pdf.

4. Indonesia's website containing information on MAP and APAs also explains the consultation process put in place to be applied when Indonesia's competent authority considers a MAP request to be inadmissible or where the objection raised in that request is not justified. Available at: www.pajak.go.id/apa-map, under paragraph 7.

5. Available at: www.oecd.org/tax/beps/beps-action-14-on-more-effective-dispute-resolution-peer-review-documents.pdf.

6. Available at: www.oecd.org/tax/beps/beps-action-14-on-more-effective-dispute-resolution-peer-review-documents.pdf.

7. The same information requirements are reproduced at: www.pajak.go.id/apa-map.

8. The shared public platform can be found at: www.oecd.org/ctp/dispute/country-map-profiles.htm.

References

OECD (2015a), "Making Dispute Resolution Mechanisms More Effective, Action 14 – 2015 Final Report", in *OECD/G20 Base Erosion and Profit Shifting Project*, OECD Publishing, Paris, https://dx.doi.org/10.1787/9789264241633-en.

OECD (2015b), *Model Tax Convention on Income and on Capital 2014 (Full Version)*, OECD Publishing, Paris, https://dx.doi.org/10.1787/9789264239081-en.

OECD (2017), *Model Tax Convention on Income and on Capital 2017 (Full Version)*, OECD Publishing, Paris, https://dx.doi.org/10.1787/g2g972ee-en.

Part C

Resolution of MAP cases

[C.1]   Include Article 25(2), first sentence, of the OECD Model Tax Convention in tax treaties

> Jurisdictions should ensure that their tax treaties contain a provision which requires that the competent authority who receives a MAP request from the taxpayer, shall endeavour, if the objection from the taxpayer appears to be justified and the competent authority is not itself able to arrive at a satisfactory solution, to resolve the MAP case by mutual agreement with the competent authority of the other Contracting Party, with a view to the avoidance of taxation which is not in accordance with the tax treaty.

136.   It is of critical importance that in addition to allowing taxpayers to request for a MAP, tax treaties also include the equivalent of the first sentence of Article 25(2) of the OECD Model Tax Convention (OECD, 2017), which obliges competent authorities, in situations where the objection raised by taxpayers are considered justified and where cases cannot be unilaterally resolved, to enter into discussions with each other to resolve cases of taxation not in accordance with the provisions of a tax treaty.

Current situation of Indonesia's tax treaties

137.   All but one of Indonesia's 72 tax treaties contain a provision equivalent to Article 25(2), first sentence, of the OECD Model Tax Convention requiring its competent authority to endeavour – when the objection raised is considered justified and no unilateral solution is possible – to resolve by mutual agreement with the competent authority of the other treaty partner the MAP case with a view to the avoidance of taxation which is not in accordance with the tax treaty.

138.   The remaining treaty contains a provision that is based on Article 25(2), first sentence, but also contains additional language that sets a condition for the provision to apply. This condition consists of a notification from the competent authority that received the MAP request to the other competent authority within a time limit of three years from the first notification of the action resulting in taxation not in accordance with the provisions of this Agreement. Since this provision puts an additional condition for the to apply, this treaty is not considered as having the equivalent of Article 25(2), first sentence, of the OECD Model Tax Convention.

139.   In view of this treaty, Indonesia reported that since its domestic law obliges its competent authority to notify the other competent authority of MAP requests submitted under this treaty, it would not make any practical difference on the side of Indonesia. Indonesia therefore views this provision as effectively being the equivalent of Article 25(2), first sentence, of the OECD Model Tax Convention.

Practical application

140. As was discussed under element B.1 (paragraphs 33-35), Indonesia's policy is to terminate MAP proceedings once domestic courts have issued a ruling on the case or where a hearing on the case has been finalised by the tax court. Indonesia clarified that it is because taxpayers or the tax administration could not present additional facts to the court after the hearing process is finalised, and the court decision is delivered on that basis. In such a situation, the further pursuance of the MAP case would in Indonesia's view become ineffective and could not result in a positive outcome to affect the court decision. This policy is confirmed in Article 57(3) of Regulation No. 74/2011, where it is stated that the MAP case will be terminated in case domestic court have rendered a decision.[1]

141. Three peers provided input on this issue, which is reflected in paragraphs 36-42 of this report. In their experiences, Indonesia terminates the MAP after the tax court decision was made on issues that relate or are not related to the MAP case. A fourth peer also mentioned that it is aware that Indonesia may terminate a MAP case due to domestic court cases being finalised. It further noted that it has several cases with Indonesia that are in this situation, which caused that the competent authorities could not resolve a case, because Indonesia's competent authority forced to close the case after a court hearing was concluded or after the court made a decision. The peer concluded that this resulted in severe level of double taxation for its taxpayers.

142. Article 25(2), first sentence, of the OECD Model Tax Convention clearly stipulates that competent authorities have an obligation to endeavour to resolve MAP cases with a view to come to taxation that is in accordance with the provisions of the convention. In this respect paragraph, 5.1 of the Commentary to Article 25 of the OECD Model Tax Convention clearly stipulates that this obligation entails that competent authorities are obliged to seek to resolve the case in a fair and objective manner, on its merits, in accordance with the terms of the convention and applicable principles of international law on the interpretation of treaties. While competent authorities may be bound by decisions of domestic courts for issues that are also under review in the MAP process, and which may cause that they are not able to resolve the case, the automatic termination of the case once domestic courts have rendered a decision is not in line with the obligations put on the competent authorities. Hence in such a situation this would deprive the taxpayer of relief of double taxation, whereas it could be possible that the other competent authority was able to resolve the case by providing for correlative relief.

Anticipated modifications

Multilateral Instrument

143. Indonesia signed the Multilateral Instrument. Article 16(4)(b)(i) of that instrument stipulates that Article 16(2), first sentence – containing the equivalent of Article 25(2), first sentence, of the OECD Model Tax Convention – will apply in the absence of a provision in tax treaties that is equivalent to Article 25(2), first sentence, of the OECD Model Tax Convention. In other words, in the absence of this equivalent, Article 16(4)(b)(i) of the Multilateral Instrument will modify the applicable tax treaty to include such equivalent. However, this shall only apply if both contracting parties to the applicable tax treaty have listed this treaty as a covered tax agreement under the Multilateral Instrument and insofar as both notified, pursuant to Article 16(6)(c)(i), the depositary that this treaty does not contain the equivalent of Article 25(2), first sentence, of the OECD Model Tax Convention.

144. In regard of the tax treaty identified above that is considered not to contain the equivalent of Article 25(2), first sentence, of the OECD Model Tax Convention, Indonesia did not list this treaty as a covered tax agreement under the Multilateral Instrument. Therefore, at this stage, the treaty identified above will not be modified by the Multilateral Instrument to include the equivalent of Article 25(2), first sentence, of the OECD Model Tax Convention.

Bilateral modifications

145. Indonesia reported that for the treaty that does not contain the equivalent of Article 25(2), first sentence, of the OECD Model Tax Convention and that will not be modified by the Multilateral Instrument, it intends to update it via bilateral negotiations with a view to be compliant with element C.1. Indonesia, however, has not put in place a specific plan for such negotiations nor has it taken any actions to that effect. Regardless, Indonesia reported it will seek to include Article 25(2), first sentence, of the OECD Model Tax Convention in all of its future tax treaties.

Peer input

146. All peers that provided input indicated that their treaty with Indonesia meets the requirement under element C.1, which conforms with the above analysis. For the treaty identified above that does not contain the equivalent of Article 25(2), first sentence, of the OECD Model Tax Convention, the relevant peer did not provide input.

Conclusion

	Areas for improvement	Recommendations
[C.1]	One out of 72 tax treaties does not contain a provision that is equivalent to Article 25(2), first sentence, of the OECD Model Tax Convention. This treaty will not be modified by the Multilateral Instrument to include the required provision.	As the treaty that does not contain the equivalent of Article 25(2), first sentence, of the OECD Model Tax Convention will not be modified via the Multilateral Instrument, Indonesia should follow its stated intention to request the inclusion of the required provision via bilateral negotiations.
		To this end, Indonesia should put a plan in place on how it envisages updating this treaty to include the required provision.
		In addition, Indonesia should maintain its stated intention to include the required provision in all future tax treaties.
	MAP cases are automatically terminated where domestic courts have rendered a decision on the issue for which MAP request was submitted, but also where such court decision regards the same taxpayer but is not related to an issue for which a MAP request was submitted.	Indonesia should seek to resolve all MAP cases that were accepted into the MAP process and that meet the requirements under Article 25(1) and (2) of the OECD Model Tax Convention as incorporated in Indonesia's tax treaties. In that regard, Indonesia should not automatically terminate MAP cases on the grounds that there was already a final court decision, regardless of whether such decision relates to the MAP case or not.

[C.2] Seek to resolve MAP cases within a 24-month average timeframe

> Jurisdictions should seek to resolve MAP cases within an average time frame of 24 months. This time frame applies to both jurisdictions (i.e. the jurisdiction which receives the MAP request from the taxpayer and its treaty partner).

147. As double taxation creates uncertainties and leads to costs for both taxpayers and jurisdictions, and as the resolution of MAP cases may also avoid (potential) similar issues for future years concerning the same taxpayers, it is important that MAP cases are resolved swiftly. A period of 24 months is considered as an appropriate time period to resolve MAP cases on average.

Reporting of MAP statistics

148. Statistics regarding all tax treaty related disputes concerning Indonesia are published on the website of the OECD as of 2016.[2] Indonesia also publishes "Directorate of International Taxation APA and MAP Statistics", which are available at:

www.pajak.go.id/apa-map

149. The FTA MAP Forum has agreed on rules for reporting of MAP statistics ("**MAP Statistics Reporting Framework**") for MAP requests submitted on or after 1 January 2016 ("**post-2015 cases**"). Also, for MAP requests submitted prior to that date ("**pre-2016 cases**"), the FTA MAP Forum agreed to report MAP statistics on the basis of an agreed template. Indonesia provided its MAP statistics for the years 2016-18 pursuant to the MAP Statistics Reporting Framework and within the given deadline, including all cases involving Indonesia and of which its competent authority was aware.[3] The statistics discussed below include both pre-2016 and post-2015 cases and the full statistics are attached to this report as Annex B and Annex C respectively[4] and should be considered jointly to understand the MAP caseload of Indonesia. With respect to post-2015 cases, Indonesia reported having reached out to all of its MAP partners with a view to have their MAP statistics matching. In that regard, Indonesia reported that it could match its post-2015 MAP statistics with its MAP partners. In that regard, based on the information provided by Indonesia's MAP partners, its post-2015 MAP statistics actually match those of its treaty partners as reported by the latter. [To be confirmed as to the 2018 MAP statistics].

Monitoring of MAP statistics

150. Indonesia reported that each MAP case is on a monthly bases as to the progress made to ensure that the MAP process and the target timeframe are being effectively managed. This monthly evaluation also takes into account the performance of staff handling the pending MAP cases on whether they are on track in meeting their objectives Based on this evaluation, reports are prepared, which are discussed in managerial meetings. In these meetings, next to monitoring the MAP caseload is monitored, also new cases and the fair case allocation of cases among staff is being discussed. Each section in the sub-directorate of Internal Taxation Dispute Prevention and Settlement (MAP unit) thereby has to report the progress made in resolving MAP cases.

Analysis of Indonesia's MAP caseload

Global overview

151.   The following graph shows the evolution of Indonesia's MAP caseload over the Statistics Reporting Period.

Figure C.1. **Evolution of Indonesia's MAP caseload**

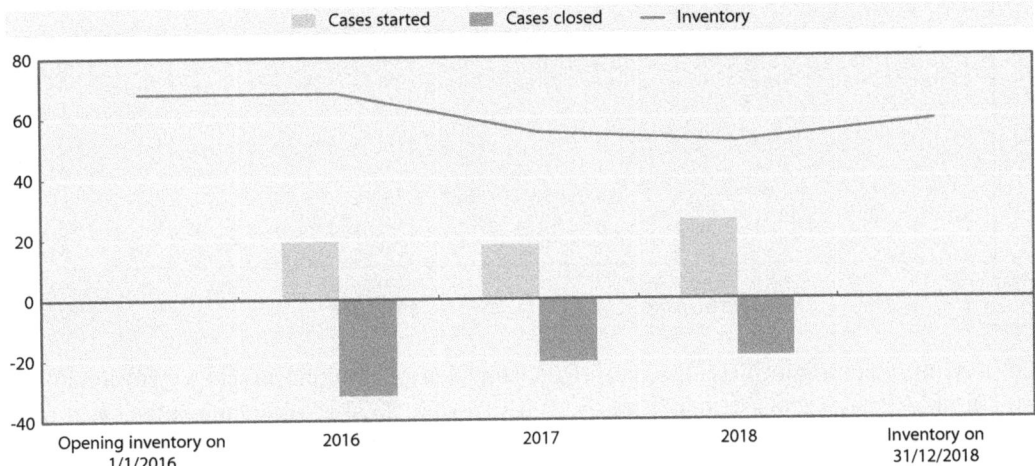

152.   At the beginning of the Statistics Reporting Period Indonesia had 68 pending MAP cases, of which 23 were attribution/allocation cases and 45 other MAP cases.[5] At the end of the Statistics Reporting Period, Indonesia had 59 MAP cases in its inventory, of which 37 are attribution/allocation cases and 22 are other MAP cases. Indonesia's MAP caseload was reduced with 13% during the Statistics Reporting Period, while attribution/allocation cases increased by 60% during the same period.

153.   The breakdown of the end inventory can be shown as follows:

Figure C.2. **End inventory on 31 December 2017 (59 cases)**

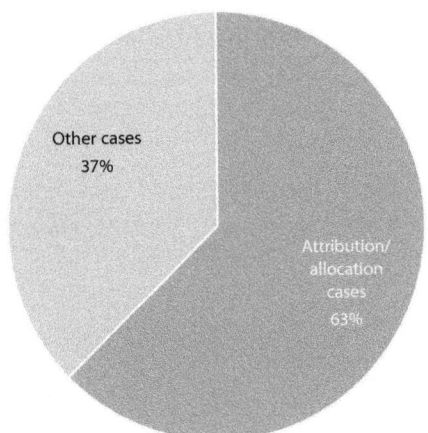

Pre-2016 cases

154.   The following graph shows the evolution of Indonesia's pre-2016 MAP cases over the Statistics Reporting Period.

Figure C.3. **Evolution of Indonesia's MAP inventory Pre-2016 cases**

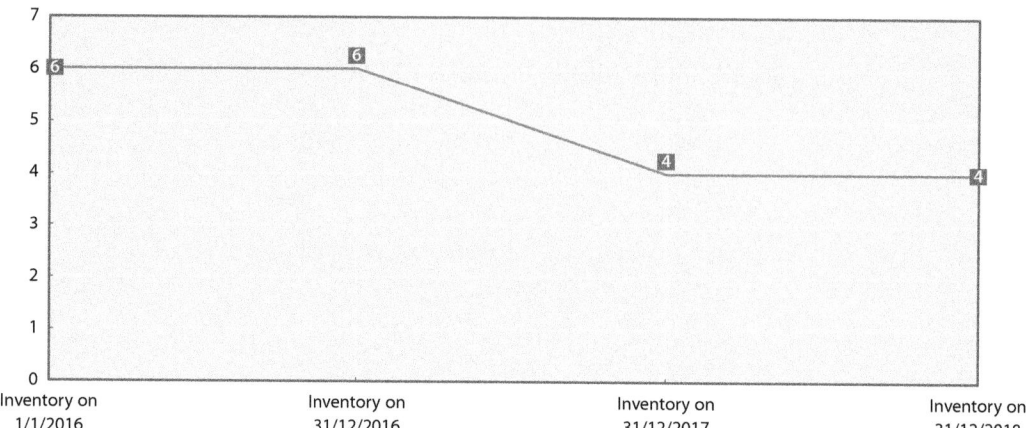

155.   At the beginning of the Statistics Reporting Period, Indonesia's MAP inventory of pre-2016 MAP cases consisted of 68 cases, of which were 23 attribution/allocation cases and 45 other cases. At the end of the Statistics Reporting Period the total inventory of pre-2016 cases had decreased to 25 cases, consisting of ten attribution/allocation cases and 15 other cases. The decrease in the number of pre-2016 MAP cases is shown in the table below.

Pre-2016 cases only	Evolution of total MAP caseload in:			Cumulative evolution of total MAP caseload over the three years (2016-18)
	2016	2017	2018	
Attribution/allocation cases	-22%	-22%	-29%	-57%
Other cases	-60%	-17%	(no cases closed)	-67%

Post-2015 cases

156.   The following graph shows the evolution of Indonesia's post-2015 MAP cases over the Statistics Reporting Period.

Figure C.4. **Evolution of Indonesia's MAP inventory Post-2015 cases**

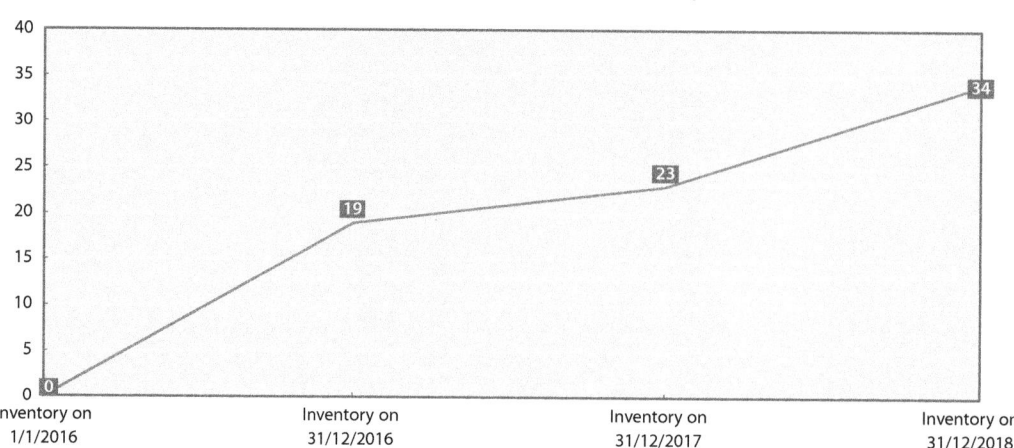

157.   In total, 63 MAP cases started during the Statistics Reporting Period, 40 of which concerned attribution/allocation cases and 23 other cases. At the end of this period the total number of post-2015 cases in the inventory was 34 cases, consisting of 27 attribution/allocation cases and seven other cases. Conclusively, Indonesia closed 29 post-2015 cases during the Statistics Reporting Period, 13 of them being attribution/allocation cases and 16 of them of them being other cases. The total number of closed cases represents 46 % of the total number of post-2015 cases that started during the Statistics Reporting Period.

158.   The number of post-2015 cases closed as compared to the number of post-2015 cases started during the Statistics Reporting Period is shown in the table below.

Post-2015 cases only	% of cases closed compared to cases started in:			Cumulative % of cases closed compared to cases started over the three years (2016-18)
	2016	2017	2018	
Attribution/allocation cases	(no cases closed)	23%	56%	33%
Other cases	(no cases closed)	220%	63%	70%

Overview of cases closed during the Statistics Reporting Period

Reported outcomes

159.   During the Statistics Reporting Period Indonesia in total closed 72 MAP cases for which the following outcomes were reported:[6]

Figure C.5. **Closed cases in 2016, 2017 or 2018 (72 cases)**

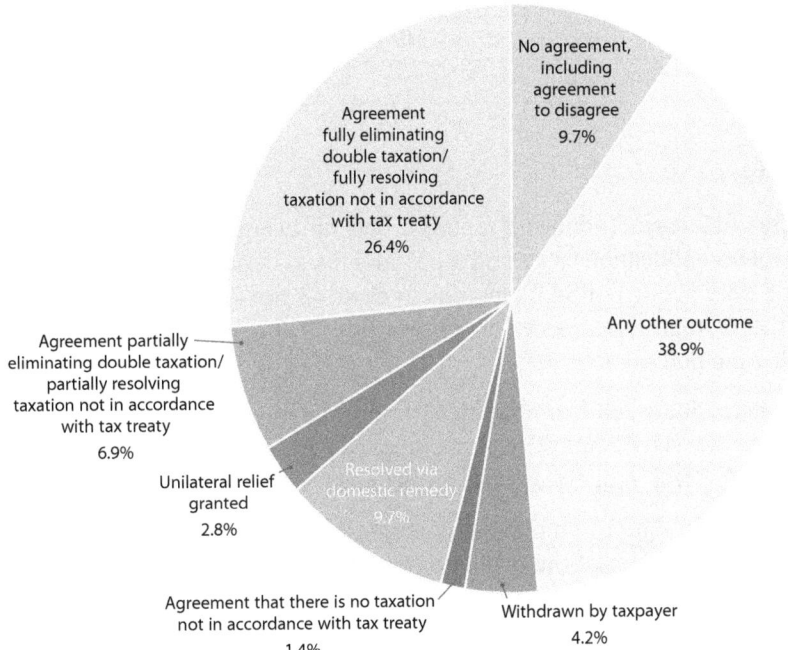

160.   This chart shows that during the Statistics Reporting Period, 19 out of 72 cases (26.4%) were closed through an agreement that fully eliminated double taxation or fully resolved taxation not in accordance with the tax treaty, and 28 (38.9%) were closed through any other outcome.

Reported outcomes for attribution/allocation cases

161.   In total, 26 attribution/allocation cases were closed during the Statistics Reporting Period. The main reported outcomes for these cases are:

- agreement fully eliminating double taxation/taxation not in accordance with the tax treaty [50%]

- resolved via domestic remedy [19%].

Reported outcomes for other cases

162.   In total, 46 other cases were closed during the Statistics Reporting Period. The main reported outcomes for these cases are:

- any other outcome [61%]

- agreement fully eliminating double taxation/taxation not in accordance with the tax treaty [13%].

Average timeframe needed to resolve MAP cases

All cases closed during the Statistics Reporting Period

163.   The average time needed to close MAP cases during the Statistics Reporting Period was 24 months. This average can be broken down as follows:

	Number of cases	Start date to End date (in months)
Attribution/Allocation cases	26	27.25
Other cases	46	22.18
All cases	72	24.00

Pre-2016 cases

164.   For pre-2016 cases Indonesia reported that on average it needed 43.37 months to close 13 attribution/allocation cases and 30.25 months to close 30 other cases. This resulted in an average time needed of 34.21 months to close 43 pre-2016 cases. For the purpose of computing the average time needed to resolve pre-2016 cases, Indonesia reported that it uses the following dates:

- Start date: one week from the date of notification by the competent authority that receives the MAP request from the taxpayer or five weeks from the receipt of the taxpayer's MAP request, whichever is the earlier date

- End date: the date of an official communication from the competent authority to inform the taxpayer of the outcome of its MAP request.

Post-2015 cases

165.   For post-2015 cases Indonesia reported that on average it needed 11.12 months to close 13 attribution/allocation cases and 7.05 months to close 16 other cases. This resulted in an average time needed of 8.87 months to close 29 post-2015 cases.

Peer input

166. The peer input in relation to resolving MAP cases will be discussed under element C.3. Specifically concerning the timely resolution of MAP cases, some peers reported that while Indonesia's competent authority is responsive and easy to contact, it also takes a long time before position papers are being issued and that this causes delay in the timely resolution of MAP cases.

Anticipated modifications

167. Indonesia reported that it is currently amending the Minister of Finance Regulation No. 240/PMK.03/2014 to *inter alia* clarify that the aim is to resolve MAP cases within a period of 24 months and to provide information on the MAP process in Indonesia.

Conclusion

	Areas for improvement	Recommendations
[C.2]	Indonesia submitted comprehensive MAP statistics on time on the basis of the MAP Statistics Reporting Framework for the years 2016, 2017 and 2018. Based on the information provided by Indonesia's MAP partners, its post-2015 MAP statistics actually match those of its treaty partners as reported by the latter. [At this stage this concerns 2016 and 2017. MAP statistics and needs to be confirmed for 2018].	
	Indonesia's MAP statistics show that during the Statistics Reporting Period it closed 46% (29 out of 63 cases) of its post-2015 cases in 8.87 months on average. In that regard, Indonesia is recommended to seek to resolve the remaining 54% of the post-2015 cases pending on 31 December 2018 (34 cases) within a timeframe that results in an average timeframe of 24 months for all post-2015 cases.	

[C.3] Provide adequate resources to the MAP function

> Jurisdictions should ensure that adequate resources are provided to the MAP function.

168. Adequate resources, including personnel, funding and training, are necessary to properly perform the competent authority function and to ensure that MAP cases are resolved in a timely, efficient and effective manner.

Description of Indonesia's competent authority

169. Under Indonesia's tax treaties the competent authority function is assigned to the Minister of Finance or its authorised representative. In this respect, Indonesia delegated, pursuant to Article 57(1) of Regulation No. 74 (2011) to the Director General of Taxes. Until April 2016 the competent authority function was in practice performed by the Director of Tax Regulation II, a sub-directorate of the Director General of Taxes. Indonesia clarified that in April 2016, the Director General of Taxes has established a specialised unit for dispute resolution under the Directorate of International Taxation, which is the sub-directorate of International Tax Dispute Prevention and Resolution ("**MAP unit**" or "**competent authority**"). This unit started with 19 staff, one of which is the head of the unit and who is authorised to exercise the competent authority function. The number of the staff has increased to 31 by the end of 2018. Apart from the head of unit, all staff members are involved in handling MAP cases.

170. With regard to the training of staff, Indonesia reported that most of the staff is trained and has experiences in dealing with international tax issues. In that regard it specified that its Director General of Taxes ensures that staff in charge of MAP cases has

sufficient experience and education in these issues and for that reason they are regularly participate in training and capacity building programmes (e.g. on transfer pricing) to improve their work performance.

171.   Further to the above, Indonesia also reported that there is adequate funding and sufficient resources for being able to handle MAP cases and conduct face-to-face meetings. This funding enables its competent authority to hold face-to-face meetings for three to four times per year with treaty partners. Given this number of possible meetings, Indonesia added that in order to avoid a late issuing of position papers, its MAP unit is adopting electronic modes of communications.

172.   Indonesia further commented that its competent authority has been facing challenges such as: (i) case complexity, (ii) difficulty in fact finding, (iii) lack of data/transparency from taxpayer, (iv) large time gap of communication with treaty partners, and (v) limited number of face-to-face meetings with other competent authorities. To tackle these challenges, Indonesia reported that it has taken the following measures:

- providing regular transfer pricing and tax treaty trainings for MAP analysts
- cross-checking with internal data, third party data, customs data, or data obtained from exchange of information
- including a domestic policy provision to provide that treaty-related disputes will be resolved within a certain timeframe
- providing better regulation for the taxpayer and the tax administration in conducting MAP process efficiently
- adapting electronic modes of communication with treaty partners
- holding monthly meetings to discuss outstanding cases, including milestones and difficulties in the attempt of resolving those cases
- scheduling consultations with treaty partners concerning outstanding cases at the beginning of the year

Monitoring mechanism

173.   Indonesia reported that each year its competent authority prepares a progress report, which includes a workload analysis. Based on this report, the Director General of Taxes decides on whether there should be any changes in the number of staff in charge of MAP cases.

Practical application

MAP statistics

174.   As discussed under element C.2, Indonesia closed its MAP cases during the Statistics Reporting Period within the pursued 24-month average. This can be illustrated by Figure C.6

175.   Based on these figures, it follows that on average it took Indonesia 24 months to close MAP cases during the Statistics Reporting Period, by which Indonesia is considered to be adequately resourced. However, for attribution/allocation cases this average was above 24 months, namely 27.25 months. This indicates that additional resources specifically dedicated to attribution/allocation cases may be necessary to accelerate the resolution of these cases.

Figure C.6. **Average time (in months) to close cases in 2016-17**

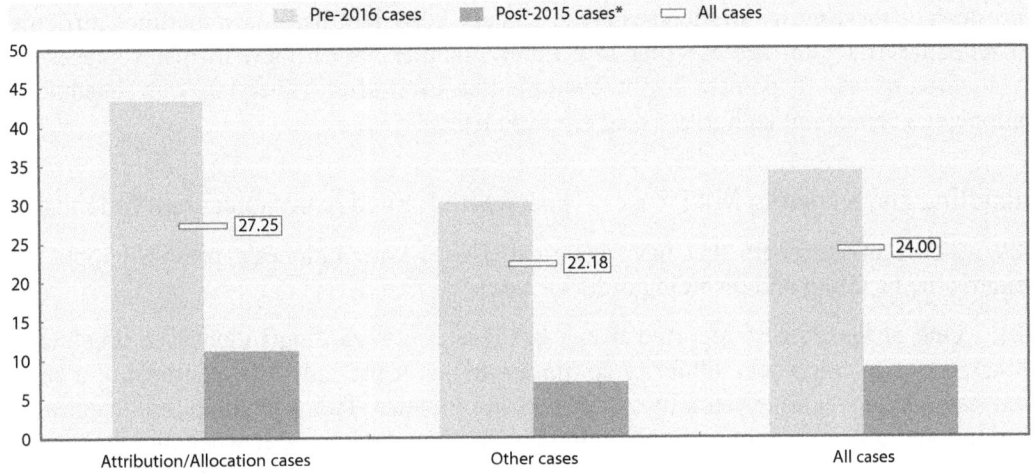

*Note that post-2015 cases only concern cases started and closed during 2016-18.

Peer input

Relationship and contacts with Indonesia's competent authority

176.   Out of the eleven peers that provided input, half of them mentioned there are not many MAP cases pending with Indonesia and thus that they have limited experiences in that regard. Six of the remaining peers considered Indonesia to be an important MAP partner, with a substantial number of MAP cases pending as compared to their inventory.

177.   Concerning the first group of peers, one peer mentioned that communications between its competent authority and that of Indonesia only started recently, for which it looks forward to a mutually beneficial and respectful relationship. Another peer noted that while it has only one MAP case with Indonesia, in its experience Indonesia's competent authority is easy to contact and answers promptly. Furthermore, one peer mentioned that due to its limited number of MAP cases with Indonesia, it has no robust working relationship concerning the handling and resolving of MAP cases and also that no face-to-face meetings have been held since 2014.

178.   Concerning the second group of peers, they all noted having a good, co-operative, or excellent working relationship with Indonesia's competent authority. With regard to communications with Indonesia's competent authority, these peers commented that they could contact it with ease or without any difficulty. One peer noted it has not encountered any barriers to communications with Indonesia's competent authority and that for all MAP cases that were initiated since 1 January 2016, Indonesia's competent authority provided prompt acknowledgement of receipt. Another peer mentioned that it values its ongoing co-operation with Indonesia and that its engagement with Indonesia's competent authority is positive and constructive with regular contact by phone and email. This peer also observed that Indonesia's competent authority is generally positive to case developments and information sharing with the peer's competent authority. The peer in particular highlighted that as a result of more frequent meetings, there has been an increase in rapport and trust with both competent authorities comfortable to express opinions and share information.

179.   Further to the above, three peers added to their input that they hold face-to-face meetings with Indonesia once or twice a year. Another peer noted that it had held one face-to-face meeting with Indonesia since January 2016, but that it is sometimes difficult to schedule a face-to-face meeting in a timely manner with a view to resolve cases in a satisfactory way. It pointed to the example that even after a meeting was scheduled, Indonesia's competent authority asked a postponement.

Handling and resolving MAP cases – peers with limited experience with Indonesia

180.   Three of the peers that have little experience with Indonesia provided input as regards the handling and resolving of MAP cases.

181.   One of these peers reported that it has concerns regarding Indonesia's timeliness of responses to competent authority communications. It presented the example of a case that has taken over four years to obtain a position paper. This peer therefore suggested that Indonesia's competent authority could prepare its position paper when an adjustment is made by Indonesia, and believes that improved communication lines could remedy this concern and would make it able to resolve MAP cases in a timelier fashion.

182.   Indonesia responded to this input and mentioned that it has a limited number of MAP cases with this peer. For the particular case being referred to by the peer, Indonesia mentioned it has provided a position paper in May 2018, but so far has not received a response from the peer's competent authority. In a reaction, the peer stressed that it indeed received the position paper, after four years. The reason that its competent authority, however, has not yet responded to the paper is that it did not contain sufficient and substantive information that would enable its competent authority to conduct a proper analysis and prepare an adequate response to Indonesia's competent authority. To obtain this information, the peer stressed its competent authority reached out to the taxpayer and upon receipt of this information it will respond to Indonesia's competent authority. As a final response, Indonesia mentioned it could definitively understand the peer's concerns, but reminded that a dedicated MAP unit was not established until 2016 and since then improvements to the MAP process were made to make it more effective. In that regard, Indonesia mentioned that for future years it is committed to provide the peer with position papers on a timely basis and also contain sufficient information.

183.   The second peer reported that it experienced no impediments to the timeliness of the resolution of MAP cases on the side of Indonesia's competent authority. While it experienced a delay in one case, this was because the taxpayer did not provide information on time. This latter was confirmed by Indonesia.

184.   Lastly, the third peer reported that some attribution/allocation cases were difficult to resolve due to lack of responsiveness by Indonesia's competent authority. In addition, this peer noted that in several non-attribution/allocation cases, the competent authorities had fundamentally different views on the interaction between Indonesia's domestic law and provisions of the treaty (for example, in determining what kind of payment constitutes a royalty). These differences created in the peer's view significant challenges in resolving MAP cases in a principled manner and within a 24-month period. The peer further mentioned that although the competent authorities sometimes communicate informally, the peer also has concerns with Indonesia competent authority's ability to respond in a timely manner. In that regard, it stressed it has experienced difficulties in communications with Indonesia's competent authority, some of which appear to have arisen when there have been turnovers in staff.

185.   Indonesia also responded to the particular input by this third peer. It noted that it acknowledges the situation raised by the peer on the issuing of and responding to position papers. It, however, has to same concern, since the peer's competent authority did not respond to position papers issued by Indonesia's competent authority. Specifically relating to the remark on the fundamentally different views on the interaction between Indonesia's domestic law and provisions of the treaty, Indonesia mentioned that it is of the view that the differences of view will not create significant challenges in resolving MAP cases in a timely manner.

186.   The peer provided for a reaction and gave an additional clarification as to its remark on the non-timely response of Indonesia's competent authority. It thereby referred to three attribution/allocation cases that could serve as an example. These are:

- In one case Indonesia's competent authority issued a position paper in 2014 involving multiple years. However, since for some of these years court cases were pending in Indonesia, the peer's competent authority asked to postpone the closing of these years until the court had rendered a decision on the case, to which Indonesia's competent authority agreed. The taxpayer subsequently submitted a MAP request for additional years pertaining to the same case, for which Indonesia issued a position paper in December 2018, and to which the peer's competent authority is currently preparing a response.

- In the second case the peer's competent authority requested Indonesia in 2015 to provide a position paper, which was not issued until August 2018. The peer is currently preparing a response.

- In the third case, the peer mentioned that Indonesia's competent agreed after a face-to-face meeting that was held in 2014 to provide a written explanation addressing how its domestic law interacts with treaties and Indonesia's obligations arising from these treaties. This explanation was not received until early 2019, for which the peer is currently preparing a response.

187.   The peer further noted that it is unaware of any cases in which its competent authority has committed to provide a response to Indonesia's position papers and has not done so either. In the peer's opinion, these differences in views underscores that communication is an area in which both competent authorities could work better to improve the resolution of MAP cases.

188.   As a last reaction, Indonesia expressed that it shares the same views as the peer that their competent authorities should improve the communication in order to reach a resolution of their mutual MAP cases. It also understands that it has been a long time since their competent authorities conducted a face-to-face meeting, for which it hopes such a meeting can be scheduled in the foreseeable future. With respect to the cases being referred to by the peer, Indonesia mentioned that it already sent two emails to the peer's competent authority in December 2018 and April 2019, in which it clearly explained the pending MAP inventory and follow up on its position set out in the position papers that were distributed previously. In Indonesia's view, the peer's competent authority could respond to those emails to clarify the matter if there are any difference of views as to the substance of the case. Apart from this issue, Indonesia mentioned it looks forward to a better and productive co-operation between their competent authorities.

Handling and resolving MAP cases – peers with more experience with Indonesia

189. For those peers that have more experience in handling and resolving MAP cases with Indonesia, one peer mentioned that it had until 2016 not resolved MAP cases with Indonesia, but that since then there was an improvement, especially due to more personal contact through face-to-face meetings. Current experiences lead for this peer to the conclusion that treaty obligations related to the MAP process are fully implemented in good faith and MAP cases are resolved in a timely manner.

190. Another peer reported that it understood that cases are processed by regional offices in Indonesia, which often prioritise cases by revenue, not by age. In this peer's view it can delay the resolution of cases. A third peer also mentioned that it experienced some delays in the MAP process with Indonesia.

191. Further to the above, one peer also noted reported that it is usual that Indonesia's competent authority did not present written position papers on Indonesian-initiated, but explained the position verbally during the face-to-face. This peer regards preparations and exchanges of position papers in a timely manner as the most important elements for the timely and effective resolution of MAP cases, as without such papers the treaty partner would face difficulties in identifying the issues of the case under review and presenting resolution for cases, which causes difficulties to the MAP process. The peer therefore expects that both competent authorities make every effort to proceed discussions in a constructive and productive way by mutually presenting and explaining their own positions and supporting facts and circumstances of the pending MAP cases. The peer concluded by stating that it would appreciate if Indonesia could share the same understanding and make every efforts at improving the situation for the timely and effective resolution of MAP cases in line with the minimum standard of BEPS Action 14.

192. Concerning the input from the peer reflected in the previous paragraph and with respect to the statement that position papers were not presented in written form, Indonesia responded and mentioned that this issue has not occurred anymore within the last two years.

193. The relevant peer provided a reaction and stated that it cannot understand the rationale behind Indonesia's argumentation. It pointed to the period 2016-18, in which its competent authority and that of Indonesia discussed nine new MAP attribution/ allocation cases and four APA cases via face-to-face meetings. Apart from one case, the peer's competent authority did not receive any position paper from Indonesia's competent authority for these APA cases before these meetings. Furthermore, the peer mentioned that for the one case where a position paper was presented, its content was insufficient as it did not include essential information on the case and Indonesia's position. As regards the MAP cases, the peer also mentioned that it only received position papers for two cases before the first face-to-face meeting in which the case was to be discussed. Also these position papers lacked important information. In addition, the peer reiterated its earlier input in that its competent authority rarely receives position papers from Indonesia before the first face-to-face meeting of each case, and even when position papers were presented before these meetings, substantial information for resolving the case was never included. In fact, according to the peer, during these meetings Indonesia's competent authority held the position that they would present this information only if the peer's competent authority accepted Indonesia's transfer pricing method beforehand. The peer concluded by stating that practice in Indonesia is positively changing, as Indonesia's competent authority strives at improving the situation by endeavouring to present written position papers in advance of face-to-face meetings. Although the peer still recognised that improvement could be made

as regards the content of the position papers, it highly values such positive sign. It further mentioned it would appreciate if Indonesia's competent authority continues its endeavours to present their position papers with sufficient information in a timely manner in order to ensure timely resolution of their mutual MAP cases.

194.   Indonesia provided a final response to this reaction. It mentioned that for the case where the peer stated that it would have required upfront approval as to the used transfer pricing method, it was due to some missing information that its competent authority it could not provide their position in full as to which transfer pricing method should be applied and the rationale behind it. Furthermore, it also referred to one case that was discussed during a face-to-face meeting where the adjustment under review was made by the peer, following which it concluded that the peer's competent authority should provide the position paper and not that of Indonesia, which it also communicated through a notification letter to the peer. The peer's competent authority, however, held the opposite view. In addition, Indonesia mentioned that in some MAP cases, the peer's competent authority also presented its position very briefly, thereby usually confirming the taxpayer's proposal on how to resolve the case and without supporting arguments why this proposal was adopted. Nevertheless, Indonesia agreed in a general sense with the peer's input regarding the (timely) issuing of position papers. It added that it will endeavour to present these with sufficient information and in due time prior to face-to-face meetings, such with a view to ensure a timely resolution of MAP cases.

Suggestions for improvement

195.   In addition to the input presented above, five peers made suggestions for improvement. One of these peers suggested that Indonesia's competent authority holds regular meetings with other jurisdictions to ensure that there is a consistent progress on MAP cases. The second peer, whose suggestion was also partially reflected in paragraph 180 above, suggested that where the case under review concerns an adjustment made by Indonesia, it could prepare a position paper in due time to explain the basis for its adjustments, including: (i) the factors considered in the application of the arm's length principle, (ii) an economic analysis that discusses comparability and comparables, and (iii) the rationale for the selection of the most appropriate transfer pricing methodology and the profit level indicator. A third peer mentioned that improved communication between both competent authorities could improve the resolution of MAP cases on a principle basis.

196.   Further to the above, one of the three peers, whose input is reflected in paragraph 181 above, added that it would appreciate if Indonesia could improve the situation of issuing of position papers in a timely manner. The last peer mentioned it would welcome the opportunity to increase the frequency of communication through face-to-face meetings and email to facilitate timely resolution of cases. It further encourages timely notification of staffing changes within the competent authority offices and recommends that Indonesia's competent authority improves transitions when staffing changes occur so that new staff can be brought up to speed on the status of MAP cases, which will facilitate timely resolution of cases in a principled manner. Lastly, the peer mentioned that requests that Indonesia submits its position paper in a timely manner.

197.   In a general sense, Indonesia responded to the input given and mentioned that its competent authority conduct some regular face-to-face meetings with its main MAP counterparts to ensure the timely resolution of MAP cases. Also it will endeavour to provide a position paper within sufficient information and analysis on a timely basis.

Anticipated modifications

198.   Indonesia indicated that it does not anticipate any modifications in relation to element C.3.

Conclusion

	Areas for improvement	Recommendations
[C.3]	Although MAP cases were closed within 24 months on average (which is the pursued average for resolving MAP cases received on or after 1 January 2016), peers indicated that they experienced several difficulties in resolving MAP cases, which concerns: • scheduling of face-to-face meetings • obtaining positions papers in due time (and before a face-to-face meeting) and with a substantial information on the case and an analysis and explanation of the competent authority's position • receiving responses to position papers issued by peers and receiving timely responses to communications on pending MAP cases. Therefore, there is a risk that pending post-2015 cases will in the future not be resolved within the pursued average of 24 months and this might indicate that the available resources for Indonesia's competent authority are not adequately used.	Indonesia should ensure that resources available for the competent authority function are adequately used in order to resolve MAP cases in a timely, efficient and effective manner. In this respect Indonesia should ensure that such adequate use enables its competent authority to: • more frequently hold face-to-face meetings • issue position papers in due time and include in those papers substantial information on the case and an analysis and explanation of the Indonesia's position • respond to position papers issued by competent authorities of the treaty partners and respond to communications on pending MAP cases with these partners in a timely manner. Furthermore, as Indonesia resolved attribution/allocation cases in 27.25 months on average, it could consider devoting current available resources to these cases in order to accelerate their resolution.

[C.4]   Ensure staff in charge of MAP has the authority to resolve cases in accordance with the applicable tax treaty

> Jurisdictions should ensure that the staff in charge of MAP processes have the authority to resolve MAP cases in accordance with the terms of the applicable tax treaty, in particular without being dependent on the approval or the direction of the tax administration personnel who made the adjustments at issue or being influenced by considerations of the policy that the jurisdictions would like to see reflected in future amendments to the treaty.

199.   Ensuring that staff in charge of MAP can and will resolve cases, absent any approval/ direction by the tax administration personnel directly involved in the adjustment and absent any policy considerations, contributes to a principled and consistent approach to MAP cases.

Functioning of staff in charge of MAP

200.   Indonesia reported that upon receipt of a MAP request, it is being assigned to staff within the competent authority, which further handles the case. To this Indonesia added that MAP analysts may hold discussions and receive recommendations from related units within the Directorate General of Tax, if necessary. For example, Indonesia has a Quality Assurance Team, which provides consultation and assures the quality of position papers exchanged during MAP. Furthermore, Indonesia clarified that once its MAP team enters into face-to-face meetings with other competent authorities, it has full authority to make decisions related to MAP.

201.   Further to the above, Indonesia reported that when its competent authority reaches an agreement with the other competent authority concerned, such MAP agreement is final and no further approval is necessary outside the competent authority. In this

respect and concerning the independent functioning of staff in charge of MAP from the audit department, Indonesia stated that staff in charge of MAP in practice operates independently and has the authority to resolve MAP cases without being dependent on the approval and/or direction by the auditor who made the adjustment at issue or other external sources. Indonesia clarified that the audit function is performed at the level of local and regional tax offices, which report to a different directorate, namely the Directorate of Audit and Collection, which is a sub-directorate of the Directorate General of Taxes.

202. Article 22 of Regulation No. 240/PMK.03/2014 lists the actions and activities staff in charge of MAP cases may pursue, which among others are holding discussions with taxpayers and preparing a position paper. In addition, Article 23 and 24 define the process for issuing of these papers. Article 25 further prescribes the process for communicating with the other competent authorities, which refers to electronic communication and face-to-face meetings, and which persons are allowed to conduct these communications.

203. Further to the above, Indonesia reported that the resolution of MAP cases is not influenced by any policy considerations. It is also independent from treaty negotiation function.

Practical application

204. Peers that provided input generally reported no impediments in Indonesia to perform its MAP function in the absence of approval or the direction of the tax administration personnel who made the adjustments at issue or being influenced by considerations of the policy. Two peers, however, reported such impediments.

205. One of these peers reported that in its view staff in charge of MAP in Indonesia is required to obtain an approval for MAP outcomes at a very senior level, which serves as a bottle neck in the process and which can contribute to delays. This peer further mentioned it believes that such decision makers include representatives of the audit functions and that this may affect the independence of Indonesia's competent authority function. This peer therefore suggested that Indonesia's competent authority should be given independence to make its decisions without requiring approvals at a higher level in the organisation. This in particular concerns no longer requiring approval from representatives of the audit function for outcome of MAP discussions. Indonesia responded to the input given and mentioned that it the decision in MAP is fully taken by the competent authority, which is located in the head office of the Director General of Taxes. Input from the Quality Assurance Team, described in paragraph 200 above, could be taken into account, but Indonesia stressed that the input from this team is not binding in nature. Also audit functions may convey their inputs on the case, but in all circumstances the decision on a MAP case is solely to be made by the competent authority. The peer reacted to this response and mentioned that local tax offices often hold records and information that are required by the competent authority. The obtaining of this information could in the peer's view delay the resolution of MAP cases. Furthermore, the peer mentioned that the Directorate General of Taxes obtains input and advice on MAP cases from a panel of senior tax officials, which include representatives of the audit function. In the peer's view this may result in a bottleneck in the process and which can cause delays. Indonesia, in turn, mentioned it could understand the peer's concern about the bottleneck issue and appreciate the input given. It further mentioned that it will endeavour to resolve the issue in the future.

206. The second peer noted that during a MAP meeting in 2016, Indonesian auditors were present, to present facts related to the case (the case concerned the attribution of profits to a permanent establishment). In the peer's view the auditors took a very aggressive position

and were also very insistent on their position. As a result hereof, the peer was not able to reach a solution for the case under review, which left the taxpayer with a severe level of double taxation.

207. Indonesia also responded to this input and mentioned that during face-to-face meetings with this particular peer, Indonesia has never involved officers from local tax offices. In one meeting, however, Indonesia clarified that its competent authority invited personnel from the audit department, but these persons were not auditors and were only invited to respond to the situation where the peer brought auditors to the face-to-face meeting. In a more general sense, Indonesia stressed that its competent authority has done its best endeavours to be independent and to resolve the case fairly.

208. The peer provided a reaction to Indonesia's response and mentioned that it was not fully aware of the status of the personnel that as present at a face-to-face meeting. It further explained that as all of its pending MAP cases with Indonesia concern Indonesian-based adjustments, the peer's competent authority did not bring auditors to such face-to-face meetings. The peer also explained that in one meeting a local tax officer attended the meeting, who was familiar with the taxpayer, but this was only for fact-finding and training purposes. To this the peer added, that its initial input was to reflect that Indonesia takes very aggressive positons, whereby it was also not possible to resolve cases due to decisions of domestic courts. Taking this altogether, the peer is of the view that there is no possibility for taxpayers to have their cases of double taxation resolved. If MAP cases would be dealt with more quickly, it would be possible to actually reach an agreement before the court has rendered its decision, by which Indonesia's competent authority would no longer be in a position to enter into an agreement that deviates from this position.

Anticipated modifications

209. Indonesia indicated that it does not anticipate any modifications in relation to element C.4.

Conclusion

	Areas for improvement	Recommendations
[C.4]	-	As it has done thus far, Indonesia should continue to ensure that its competent authority has the authority, and uses that authority in practice, to resolve MAP cases without being dependent on approval or direction from the tax administration personnel directly involved in the adjustment at issue and absent any policy considerations that Indonesia would like to see reflected in future amendments to the treaty.

[C.5] Use appropriate performance indicators for the MAP function

Jurisdictions should not use performance indicators for their competent authority functions and staff in charge of MAP processes based on the amount of sustained audit adjustments or maintaining tax revenue.

210. For ensuring that each case is considered on its individual merits and will be resolved in a principled and consistent manner, it is essential that any performance indicators for the competent authority function and for the staff in charge of MAP processes are appropriate

and not based on the amount of sustained audit adjustments or aim at maintaining a certain amount of tax revenue.

Performance indicators used by Indonesia

211. Indonesia reported that the Directorate General of Taxes has implemented key performance indicators, which include the number of resolved MAP cases and time taken to resolve a MAP case. These indicators are evaluated on an annual basis. Indonesia further reported that its competent authority also evaluates each MAP cases as to their progress, such to ensure that the MAP process and the target timeframe are being effectively managed. This monthly evaluation also takes into account the performance of staff handling the pending MAP cases on whether they are on track in meeting their objectives Based on this evaluation, reports are prepared, which are discussed in managerial meetings.

212. The Action 14 Final Report (OECD, 2015) includes examples of performance indicators that are considered appropriate. These indicators are shown below and presented in the form of a checklist:

- ☑ number of MAP cases resolved

- ☐ consistency (i.e. a treaty should be applied in a principled and consistent manner to MAP cases involving the same facts and similarly-situated taxpayers)

- ☑ time taken to resolve a MAP case (recognising that the time taken to resolve a MAP case may vary according to its complexity and that matters not under the control of a competent authority may have a significant impact on the time needed to resolve a case).

213. Further to the above, Indonesia reported that it does not use any performance indicators for staff in charge of MAP that are related to the outcome of MAP discussions in terms of the amount of sustained audit adjustments or maintained tax revenue. In other words, staff in charge of MAP is not evaluated on the basis of the material outcome of MAP discussions.

Practical application

214. Peers provided no specific input relating to this element of the Action 14 Minimum Standard.

Anticipated modifications

215. Indonesia indicated that it does not anticipate any modifications in relation to element C.5.

Conclusion

	Areas for improvement	Recommendations
[C.5]	-	As it has done thus far, Indonesia should continue to use appropriate performance indicators.

[C.6] Provide transparency with respect to the position on MAP arbitration

> Jurisdictions should provide transparency with respect to their positions on MAP arbitration.

216. The inclusion of an arbitration provision in tax treaties may help ensure that MAP cases are resolved within a certain timeframe, which provides certainty to both taxpayers and competent authorities. In order to have full clarity on whether arbitration as a final stage in the MAP process can and will be available in jurisdictions it is important that jurisdictions are transparent on their position on MAP arbitration.

Position on MAP arbitration

217. Indonesia reported that it has no domestic mechanism for applying arbitration procedures in relation to the MAP process, other than for the one treaty that contains a provision hereto (see below). Indonesia further specified that its treaty policy is not to include a mandatory and binding arbitration provision in its bilateral tax treaties. In this respect, in the Commentary of non-members to the 2017 OECD Model Tax Convention, Indonesia reserved the right not to include paragraph 5 of Article 25 in its tax treaties. Indonesia's position on MAP arbitration, however, is not clearly reflected in its MAP profile.

Practical application

218. Indonesia has incorporated one arbitration clause in one of its tax treaties as a final stage to the MAP, which provides for a voluntary arbitration procedure.

Anticipated modifications

219. Indonesia indicated that it does not anticipate any modifications in relation to element C.6.

Conclusion

	Areas for improvement	Recommendations
[C.6]	No correct specification in the MAP profile on whether there are any legal limitations in its domestic law to include MAP arbitration in tax treaties.	Indonesia should correctly specify in its MAP profile whether there are any legal limitations in its domestic law to include MAP arbitration in tax treaties.

Notes

1. See also www.pajak.go.id/apa-map, paragraph 6.

2. Available at: www.oecd.org/tax/dispute/mutual-agreement-procedure-statistics.htm. These statistics are up to and include fiscal year 2017.

3. Indonesia's 2016 and 2017 MAP statistics were corrected in the course of its peer review and deviate from the published MAP statistics for 2016 and 2017. See further explanations in Annex B and Annex C.

4. For post-2015 cases, if the number of MAP cases in Indonesia's inventory at the beginning of the Statistics Reporting Period plus the number of MAP cases started during the Statistics Reporting Period was more than five, Indonesia reports its MAP caseload on a jurisdiction-by-jurisdiction basis. This rule applies for each type of cases (attribution/allocation cases and other cases).

5. For pre-2016 and post-2015 cases, Indonesia follows the MAP Statistics Reporting Framework for determining whether a case is considered an attribution/allocation MAP case. Annex D of MAP Statistics Reporting Framework provides that "an attribution/allocation MAP case is a MAP case where the taxpayer's MAP request relates to (i) the attribution of profits to a permanent establishment (see e.g. Article 7 of the OECD Model Tax Convention); or (ii) the determination of profits between associated enterprises (see e.g. Article 9 of the OECD Model Tax Convention), which is also known as a transfer pricing MAP case".

6. There are 26 cases closed with the outcome of "any other outcome". These cases all relate to the application of branch profit tax of permanent establishment. As the competent authorities could not reach an agreement as to whether these cases fall into the scope of the treaty, and they were closed without any agreements.

References

OECD (2015), "Making Dispute Resolution Mechanisms More Effective, Action 14 – 2015 Final Report", in *OECD/G20 Base Erosion and Profit Shifting Project*, OECD Publishing, Paris, https://dx.doi.org/10.1787/9789264241633-en.

OECD (2017), *Model Tax Convention on Income and on Capital 2017 (Full Version)*, OECD Publishing, Paris, https://dx.doi.org/10.1787/g2g972ee-en.

Part D

Implementation of MAP agreements

[D.1] Implement all MAP agreements

> Jurisdictions should implement any agreement reached in MAP discussions, including by making appropriate adjustments to the tax assessed in transfer pricing cases.

220.   In order to provide full certainty to taxpayers and the jurisdictions, it is essential that all MAP agreements are implemented by the competent authorities concerned.

Legal framework to implement MAP agreements

221.   Indonesia reported that has a domestic statute of limitation for both upward and downward adjustments regarding the implementation of MAP agreements. This statute of limitation is five years as from the end of the taxable year. However, where a tax treaty contains the second sentence of Article 25(2) of the OECD Model Tax Convention (OECD, 2017), Indonesia reported it will always implement MAP agreements regardless of the statute of limitation.

222.   Concerning the process for implementing MAP agreements, Indonesia referred to Article 27(3) of the Minister of Finance Regulation No. 240/PMK.03/2014, where it is stated that before a MAP agreement will be finalised, the Director General of Taxes has to request the taxpayer for confirmation on its acceptance or non-acceptance of the agreement. Article 27(4) specifies that taxpayers have to give their confirmation in writing. Upon receipt of such confirmation, the MAP agreement will, pursuant to Article 27(5) be finalised.[1] In this respect, Indonesia reported that when in practice its competent authority is already aware of the taxpayer's consent beforehand or where such consent is not necessary (e.g. in cases of MAP agreements of a general nature), the tax administration can immediately implement MAP agreements without the need to await a formal confirmation.[2]

223.   Further to the above, Article 28 of the Minister of Finance Regulation No. 240/PMK.03/2014 defines the subsequent process for implementing MAP agreements, where it is stipulated that the Director General of Taxes will issue a decree that confirms the MAP agreement and the follow-up thereof, as well as that taxpayers will be notified thereof. The local tax offices will then on that basis implement the agreement. Article 29 of the regulation defines in detail how MAP agreements will be implemented, which is dependent on the type of adjustments that have to be made.

Practical application

224.   As to the monitoring of the implementation of MAP agreements, Indonesia reported that the Directorate General of Taxes ensures that the local tax offices will take the necessary measures to implement the agreements. In this regard, local tax offices have to report back to the competent authority once the MAP agreement has been implemented. In this respect, Indonesia reported that all MAP agreements that were reached on or after since 1 January 2016, once accepted by taxpayer, have been (or will be) implemented.

225.   All but one peers that provided input indicated that they were not aware of any MAP agreement reached on or after 1 January 2016 that was not implemented by Indonesia. One of these peers mentioned that to date it has not reached any MAP agreement with Indonesia, while another peer stated that it has reached two MAP agreements with Indonesia since 1 January 2016, but that these agreement did not require an implementation in Indonesia, following which the peer concluded that it cannot make comments whether Indonesia has implemented MAP agreements appropriately and in a timely manner.

226.   The remaining peer mentioned that while its treaty with Indonesia contains the equivalent of Article 25(2), second sentence, of the OECD Model Tax Convention, it has encountered challenges with the implementation of MAP agreements by Indonesia due to domestic time limits. This peer mentioned that in Indonesia a domestic time limit of five years applies, starting from the taxable year in which an adjustment was made. The peer further mentioned that this statute of limitation is being applied differently, such depending on whether the MAP case relates to an adjustment made by Indonesia or its treaty partner. To clarify the matter, this peer presented an example of a MAP case that was initiated by the peer's competent authority in 2013 and which related to an adjustment made by the peer's tax administration. In January 2018, both competent authorities agreed to start discussions on the case. However, Indonesia's domestic statute of limitation of five years expired on 31 December 2018, following which there was insufficient time for the competent authorities to discuss and resolve the case. On the contrary, according to this peer, cases that concern an adjustment made by Indonesia are not subject to such five-year time limit, following which a case that was initiated in 2008 is still under discussion. This peer therefore considered that the time limit is being unfairly applied to adjustments made by treaty partners and that it may limit a sufficient and in-depth discussions for resolving such cases. Furthermore, the peer noted that it is deeply concerned that this time limit may preclude taxpayers' access to MAP when a treaty partner makes an adjustment in the taxable year which is already beyond Indonesia's five-year limit. This peer believes that this limitation is contrary to the treaty obligation and the Action 14 Minimum Standard, especially since its treaty with Indonesia contains the equivalent of Article 25(2), second sentence, of the OECD Model Tax Convention.

227.   Indonesia responded to the input given by the second peer and mentioned that Article 25(2), second sentence, does not oblige jurisdictions to disregard its domestic statutory time limits, but requires jurisdictions to implement MAP agreements reached. It further mentioned that the issue does not relate to access to MAP, since Indonesia will grant such access even if the five-year statute of limitation has passed.

Anticipated modifications

228.   Indonesia indicated that it does not anticipate any modifications in relation to element D.1.

Conclusion

	Areas for improvement	Recommendations
[D.1]	As will be discussed under element D.3, not all of Indonesia's tax treaties contain the equivalent of Article 25(2), second sentence, of the OECD Model Tax Convention. Therefore, there is a risk that for those tax treaties that do not contain that provision, not all MAP agreements will be implemented due to time limits of five years in its domestic law. This regards only cases where the adjustment under review is made at the level of the treaty partner, while such is not the case for domestic adjustments.	When, after a MAP case is initiated, the domestic statute of limitation may, in the absence of the second sentence of Article 25(2) of the OECD Model Tax Convention in Indonesia's relevant tax treaty, prevent the implementation of a MAP agreement when the adjustment is made at the level of the treaty partner, Indonesia should put appropriate procedures in place to ensure that such an agreement is implemented. In addition, where during the MAP process the domestic statute of limitations may expire and may then affect the possibility to implement a MAP agreement, Indonesia should for clarity and transparency purposes notify the treaty partner thereof without delay.

[D.2] Implement all MAP agreements on a timely basis

Agreements reached by competent authorities through the MAP process should be implemented on a timely basis.

229. Delays in implementing MAP agreements may lead to adverse financial consequences for both taxpayers and competent authorities. To avoid this and to increase certainty for all parties involved, it is important that the implementation of any MAP agreement is not obstructed by procedural and/or statutory delays in the jurisdictions concerned.

Theoretical timeframe for implementing mutual agreements

230. Indonesia reported that it currently does not have specific timeframes in place regarding the implementation of MAP agreements. However, in practice, the Directorate General of Taxes issues the required decree by no later than a month from the date the of: (i) the acceptance of a written notification from the other competent authority stating that the MAP agreement can be implemented; and (ii) Indonesia's notification to the other competent authority stating the same.

Practical application

231. Indonesia reported that all MAP agreements that were reached on or after since 1 January 2016, once accepted by taxpayers, have been (or will be) implemented and that no cases of noticeable delays have occurred.

232. All but one peers that provided input have not indicated experiencing any problems with regard to timeliness of the implementation of MAP agreements reached. The remaining peer mentioned that in 2017 it entered for some cases into MAP agreements with Indonesia, but for which Indonesia's competent authority indicated that the outcome could not yet be implemented due to the fact that certain tax declaration forms first have to be adjusted.

233. To this input Indonesia responded that it has found the best solution to settle these issues, such by applying a new additional form specifically dedicated to implement the MAP agreement. This solution was communicated to the peer's competent authority and the relevant taxpayers.

Anticipated modifications

234.   Indonesia reported that it is in the process of amending the Minister of Finance Regulation No. 240/PMK.03/2014 to specify the timelines that should be applied for implementing MAP agreements, which are currently used in practice. This timeline will stipulate that the Directorate General of Taxes will issue the decree for the implementation of the agreement by no later than a month from the date of: (i) the acceptance of a written notification from the other competent authority stating that the MAP agreement can be implemented; and (ii) Indonesia's notification to the other competent authority stating the same.

Conclusion

	Areas for improvement	Recommendations
[D.2]	-	As it has done thus far, Indonesia should continue to implement all MAP agreements on a timely basis if the conditions for such implementation are fulfilled.

[D.3]   Include Article 25(2), second sentence, of the OECD Model Tax Convention in tax treaties or alternative provisions in Article 9(1) and Article 7(2)

> Jurisdictions should either (i) provide in their tax treaties that any mutual agreement reached through MAP shall be implemented notwithstanding any time limits in their domestic law, or (ii) be willing to accept alternative treaty provisions that limit the time during which a Contracting Party may make an adjustment pursuant to Article 9(1) or Article 7(2), in order to avoid late adjustments with respect to which MAP relief will not be available.

235.   In order to provide full certainty to taxpayers it is essential that implementation of MAP agreements is not obstructed by any time limits in the domestic law of the jurisdictions concerned. Such certainty can be provided by either including the equivalent of Article 25(2), second sentence, of the OECD Model Tax Convention in tax treaties, or alternatively, setting a time limit in Article 9(1) and Article 7(2) for making adjustments to avoid that late adjustments obstruct granting of MAP relief.

Legal framework and current situation of Indonesia's tax treaties

236.   As discussed under element D.1, Indonesia has a statute of limitation for implementing MAP agreements, which is five years and regards both upward and downward adjustments.

237.   Out of Indonesia's 72 tax treaties, 17 contain a provision that equivalent to Article 25(2), second sentence, of the OECD Model Tax Convention that any mutual agreement reached through MAP shall be implemented notwithstanding any time limits in their domestic law. Furthermore, three tax treaties contain the alternative provisions in Article 9(1) and Article 7(2) or in their MAP article, setting a time limit for making adjustments and one contains only the alternative provision for Article 9(1).

238.   The remaining 51 treaties can be categorised as follows:

- 47 treaties neither contain a provision that is equivalent to Article 25(2), second sentence, of the OECD Model Tax Convention nor any of the provisions Eight treaties neither contain nor any of the alternative provisions for Article 9(1) and 7(2) setting a time limits for making transfer pricing adjustments.

- Two treaties contain a provision setting a time limit for the implementation of MAP agreements as provided in the domestic law of the contracting states. For this reason both treaties are considered not to contain the equivalent of Article 25(2), second sentence, of the OECD Model Tax Convention.

- Two treaties contain a provision setting a specific time limits for the implementation of MAP agreements, which is five years from the date of the MAP agreement or ten years from the end of the taxable year in which the action that led to the MAP agreement has arisen. For this reason both treaties are considered not to contain the equivalent of Article 25(2), second sentence, of the OECD Model Tax Convention.

Anticipated modifications

Multilateral Instrument

239.   Indonesia signed the Multilateral Instrument. Article 16(4)(b)(ii) of that instrument stipulates that Article 16(2), second sentence – containing the equivalent of Article 25(2), second sentence, of the OECD Model Tax Convention – will apply in the absence of a provision in tax treaties that is equivalent to Article 25(2), second sentence, of the OECD Model Tax Convention. In other words, in the absence of this equivalent, Article 16(4)(b)(ii) of the Multilateral Instrument will modify the applicable tax treaty to include such equivalent. However, this shall only apply if both contracting parties to the applicable tax treaty have listed this treaty as a covered tax agreement under the Multilateral Instrument and insofar as both, pursuant to Article 16(6)(c)(ii), notified the depositary that this treaty does not contain the equivalent of Article 25(2), second sentence, of the OECD Model Tax Convention. Article 16(4)(b)(ii) of the Multilateral Instrument will for a tax treaty not take effect if one or both of the treaty partners has, pursuant to Article 16(5)(c), reserved the right not to apply the second sentence of Article 16(2) of that instrument for all of its covered tax agreements under the condition that: (i) any MAP agreement shall be implemented notwithstanding any time limits in the domestic laws of the contracting states, or (ii) the jurisdiction intends to meet the Action 14 Minimum Standard by accepting in its tax treaties the alternative provisions to Article 9(1) and 7(2) concerning the introduction of a time limit for making transfer pricing profit adjustments.

240.   In regard of the 52 tax treaties identified above that are considered not to contain the equivalent of Article 25(2), second sentence, of the OECD Model Tax Convention or the alternative provisions for Articles 9(1) and 7(2), Indonesia listed 21 treaties as covered tax agreements under the Multilateral Instrument and for 17 of them did it make, pursuant to Article 16(6)(c)(ii), a notification that they do not contain a provision described in Article 16(4)(b)(ii). Of the relevant 17 treaty partners, two are not a signatory to the Multilateral Instrument and one did not list their treaty with Indonesia as a covered tax agreement. All of the remaining 14 treaty partners also made a notification on the basis of Article 16(6)(c)(ii). Therefore, at this stage, 14 of the 52 tax treaties identified above will be modified by the Multilateral Instrument upon its entry into force for these treaties to include the equivalent of Article 25(2), second sentence, of the OECD Model Tax Convention.

Bilateral modifications

241.   Indonesia reported that for the tax treaties that do not contain the equivalent of Article 25(2), second sentence, of the OECD Model Tax Convention or both alternatives provided for in Articles 9(1) and 7(2), and that will not be modified by the Multilateral Instrument, it will modify its notifications under Article 16(6)(d)(ii) of the Multilateral

Instrument to include ten more treaties. If done so, the expected impact hereof would be that nine of these treaties will be modified by that instrument, following which the number increases from 14 to 25. For the remaining 27 treaties, Indonesia reported that it intends to update them via bilateral negotiations with a view to be compliant with element D.3. Indonesia, however, has not put in place a specific plan for such negotiations nor has it taken any actions to that effect. Regardless, Indonesia reported it will seek to include Article 25(2), second sentence, of the OECD Model Tax Convention or both alternatives in all of its future tax treaties.

Peer input

242. Nearly all of the peers that provided input indicated that their treaty with Indonesia meets the requirement under element D.3, which conforms with the above analysis. For the 52 treaties identified that do not contain the equivalent of Article 25(2), second sentence, of the OECD Model Tax Convention, or both alternatives, three of the relevant peers provided input. Of these three, two confirmed that their treaty with Indonesia does not contain the equivalent of Article 25(2), second sentence, but that it will be modified by the Multilateral Instrument upon its entry into force for the treaty concerned, which conforms with the above analysis. The third peer also confirmed that its treaty with Indonesia does not contain the equivalent of Article 25(2), second sentence, but reported that it is willing to accept the alternative provisions setting time limits for making adjustments and that it already proposed negotiations in view of a revision of the treaty with Indonesia.

Conclusion

	Areas for improvement	Recommendations
[D.3]	52 out of 72 tax treaties contain neither a provision that is equivalent to Article 25(2), second sentence, of the OECD Model Tax Convention nor both alternative provisions provided for in Article 9(1) and Article 7(2). With respect to these 52 treaties: • 14 are expected to be modified by the Multilateral Instrument to include the required provision. • Nine are expected to be modified by the Multilateral Instrument to include the required provision, once the notifications under that instrument are modified.	Indonesia should as quickly as possible follow its stated intention and modify its notifications under the Multilateral Instrument and subsequently ratify that instrument to incorporate the equivalent to Article 25(2), second sentence, of the OECD Model Tax Convention in those 25 treaties that currently do not contain such equivalent and that will be modified by the Multilateral Instrument upon its entry into force for the treaties concerned. For 26 of the remaining 27 treaties that will not be modified by the Multilateral Instrument to include the equivalent of Article 25(2), second sentence, of the OECD Model Tax Convention, Indonesia should follow its stated intention to request the inclusion of the required provision via bilateral negotiations or be willing to accept the inclusion of both alternative provisions. To this end, Indonesia should put a plan in place on how it envisages updating these 26 treaties to include the required provision or its alternative. For the remaining treaty, Indonesia should enter into discussions with the relevant treaty partner following their invitations to open negotiations with a view to include such provision or both of alternative provisions. In addition, Indonesia should maintain its stated intention to include the required provision, or be willing to accept the inclusion of both alternatives provisions, in all future tax treaties.

Notes

1. See also www.pajak.go.id/apa-map, paragraphs 12-15.

2. This is also clarified in Article 57(5) and (6) of Regulation No. 74 (2011), where the Director General of Taxes is allowed to implement a MAP agreement ex officio in certain circumstances.

Reference

OECD (2017), *Model Tax Convention on Income and on Capital 2017 (Full Version)*, OECD Publishing, Paris, https://dx.doi.org/10.1787/g2g972ee-en.

Summary

	Areas for improvement	Recommendations
	Part A: Preventing disputes	
[A.1]	Three out of 72 tax treaties do not contain a provision that is equivalent to Article 25(3), first sentence, of the OECD Model Tax Convention. While currently none of these three treaties will be modified by the Multilateral Instrument to include the required provision, such effect is anticipated for two of these three treaties when notifications under that instrument are modified.	Indonesia should as quickly as possible follow its stated intention and modify its notifications under the Multilateral Instrument and subsequently ratify that instrument to incorporate the equivalent of Article 25(3), first sentence, of the OECD Model Tax Convention in two of the three treaties that currently do not contain such equivalent and that will be modified by the Multilateral Instrument upon its entry into force for the treaty concerned.
		For the remaining treaty that will not be modified by the Multilateral Instrument to include the equivalent of Article 25(2), second sentence, of the OECD Model Tax Convention following its entry into force, Indonesia should request the inclusion of the required provision via bilateral negotiations.
		To this end, Indonesia should put a plan in place on how it envisages updating this treaty to include the required provision.
		In addition, Indonesia should maintain its stated intention to include the required provision in all future tax treaties.
[A.2]	Roll-back of bilateral APAs is not always available in appropriate cases and there are no clear rules available on whether such roll-backs are possible and, if so, upon what conditions.	Indonesia should follow up on its stated intention and amend regulation No. 7/PMK.03/2015 to clarify that roll-back of bilateral APAs are possible. It should in practice also allow for roll-back of bilateral APAs in all appropriate cases.
	Part B: Availability and access to MAP	
[B.1] ↓	Two out of 72 tax treaties do not contain a provision that is equivalent to Article 25(1), first sentence, of the OECD Model Tax Convention and the timeline to file a MAP request is shorter than three years from the first notification of the action resulting in taxation not in accordance with the provision of the tax treaty. Of these two treaties, one is expected to be modified by the Multilateral Instrument to include Article 25(1), second sentence.	Indonesia should as quickly as possible ratify the Multilateral Instrument to incorporate the equivalent to Article 25(1), second sentence, of the OECD Model Tax Convention in the treaty that currently does not contain such equivalent and that will be modified by the Multilateral Instrument upon its entry into force for the treaties concerned. Since this treaty will not be modified by the Multilateral Instrument as regards the first sentence of Article 25(1), Indonesia should also follow its stated intention to request the inclusion of the required provision via bilateral negotiations. This concerns a provision that is equivalent to Article 25(1), first sentence of the OECD Model Tax Convention either:
		a. as amended in the Action 14 final report; or
		b. as it read prior to the adoption of Action 14 final report, thereby including the full sentence of such provision.

	Areas for improvement	Recommendations
[B.1] ↓		Furthermore, for the other treaty that will not be modified by the Multilateral Instrument to incorporate the equivalent to Article 25(1), first and second sentence, of the OECD Model Tax Convention, Indonesia should also follow its stated intention to request the inclusion of the required provision via bilateral negotiations, which also regards one of the options identified above. To this end, Indonesia should put a plan in place on how it envisages updating this treaty to include the required provision.
	31 out of 72 tax treaties does not contain the equivalent of Article 25(1), second sentence, of the OECD Model Tax Convention, as the timeline to file a MAP request is shorter than three years from the first notification of the action resulting in taxation not in accordance with the provision of the tax treaty. With respect to these 31 treaties • Eight are expected to be modified by the Multilateral Instrument to include the required provision. • Eight are expected to be modified by the Multilateral Instrument to include the required provision, once the notifications under that instrument are modified.	Indonesia should as quickly as possible follow its stated intention and modify its notifications under the Multilateral Instrument and subsequently ratify that instrument to incorporate the equivalent to Article 25(1), second sentence, of the OECD Model Tax Convention in those 116 treaties that currently do not contain such equivalent and that will be modified by the Multilateral Instrument upon its entry into force for the treaties concerned. For the remaining 15 treaties that currently do not contain such equivalent and that will not be modified by the Multilateral Instrument to include the equivalent to Article 25(1), first sentence, of the OECD Model Tax Convention, Indonesia should follow its stated intention to request the inclusion of the required provision. To this end, Indonesia should put a plan in place on how it envisages updating these 15 treaties to include the required provision.
		In addition, Indonesia should maintain its stated intention to include Article 25(1) of the OECD Model Tax Convention in all future tax treaties.
	Access to MAP will be denied in certain cases, even when the requirements for initiating a MAP case under the treaty provision that is equivalent to Article 25(1) of the OECD Model Tax Convention are met. This in particular concerns: • cases where domestic courts have already rendered a decision on the issue for which MAP request is submitted, but also where such court decision regards the same taxpayer but is not related to an issue for which a MAP request was submitted • the requirement of filing a MAP request at the level of the treaty partner for adjustments made by Indonesia	Indonesia should ensure that access to MAP is given in all eligible cases where the requirements under Article 25(1) of the OECD Model Tax convention as incorporated in Indonesia's tax treaties have been met. In particular, Indonesia should not limit such access in cases: • where domestic courts have rendered a decision relating, or not relating, to cases for which a MAP request was submitted • where the taxpayer did not file a MAP request at the level of the treaty partner for adjustments made by Indonesia.
[B.2]	Indonesia has a documented process in place to consult the other competent authority in cases where the objection raised in the MAP request was considered as being not justified. However, it was not possible to assess whether the consultation or notification process is applied in practice because during the Review period no such cases have occurred.	
[B.3]	-	As Indonesia has thus far granted access to MAP in eligible transfer pricing cases, it should continue granting access for these cases.
[B.4]	-	As Indonesia has thus far granted access to MAP in eligible cases concerning whether the conditions for the application of a treaty anti-abuse provision have been met or whether the application of a domestic law anti-abuse provision is in conflict with the provisions of a treaty, it should continue granting access for these cases.

	Areas for improvement	Recommendations
[B.5]	-	-
[B.6]	-	As Indonesia has thus far not limited access to MAP in eligible cases when taxpayers have complied with Indonesia's information and documentation requirements for MAP requests, it should continue this practice.
[B.7]	Six out of 72 tax treaties do not contain a provision that is equivalent to Article 25(3), second sentence, of the OECD Model Tax Convention. With respect to these six treaties: • Two are expected to be modified by the Multilateral Instrument to include the required provision. • Four are expected to be modified by the Multilateral Instrument to include the required provision, once the notifications under that instrument are modified.	Indonesia should as quickly as possible follow its stated intention and modify its notifications under the Multilateral Instrument and subsequently ratify that instrument to incorporate the equivalent to Article 25(3), second sentence, of the OECD Model Tax Convention in those six treaties that currently do not contain such equivalent and that will be modified by the Multilateral Instrument upon its entry into force for the treaties concerned. In addition, Indonesia should maintain its stated intention to include the required provision in all future tax treaties.
[B.8]	-	Although not required by the Action 14 Minimum Standard, in order to further improve the level of details of its MAP guidance Indonesia could consider including information on: • whether MAP is available in cases of: (i) the application of anti-abuse provisions, (ii) multilateral disputes and (iii) bona fide foreign-initiated self-adjustments • whether taxpayers can request for the multi-year resolution of recurring issues through MAP • the consideration of interest and penalties in the MAP. Furthermore, as was suggested by a peer (reflected under element B.1), Indonesia could also consider including information how the effects of a judicial decision affects the MAP process, since taxpayers and treaty partners may not fully understand such effects.
[B.9]	-	As it has thus far made its MAP guidance available and easily accessible and published its MAP profile, Indonesia should ensure that its future updates to the MAP guidance continue to be publicly available and easily accessible and that its MAP profile published on the shared public platform is updated if needed.
[B.10]	-	-
Part C: Resolution of MAP cases		
[C.1] ↓	One out of 72 tax treaties does not contain a provision that is equivalent to Article 25(2), first sentence, of the OECD Model Tax Convention. This treaty will not be modified by the Multilateral Instrument to include the required provision.	As the treaty that does not contain the equivalent of Article 25(2), first sentence, of the OECD Model Tax Convention will not be modified via the Multilateral Instrument, Indonesia should follow its stated intention to request the inclusion of the required provision via bilateral negotiations. To this end, Indonesia should put a plan in place on how it envisages updating this treaty to include the required provision. In addition, Indonesia should maintain its stated intention to include the required provision in all future tax treaties.

		Areas for improvement	Recommendations
↓	[C.1]	MAP cases are automatically terminated where domestic courts have rendered a decision on the issue for which MAP request was submitted, but also where such court decision regards the same taxpayer but is not related to an issue for which a MAP request was submitted.	Indonesia should seek to resolve all MAP cases that were accepted into the MAP process and that meet the requirements under Article 25(1) and (2) of the OECD Model Tax Convention as incorporated in Indonesia's tax treaties. In that regard, Indonesia should not automatically terminate MAP cases on the grounds that there was already a final court decision, regardless of whether such decision relates to the MAP case or not.
	[C.2]	Indonesia submitted comprehensive MAP statistics on time on the basis of the MAP Statistics Reporting Framework for the years 2016, 2017 and 2018. Based on the information provided by Indonesia's MAP partners, its post-2015 MAP statistics actually match those of its treaty partners as reported by the latter. [At this stage this concerns 2016 and 2017. MAP statistics and needs to be confirmed for 2018]. Indonesia's MAP statistics show that during the Statistics Reporting Period it closed 46% (29 out of 63 cases) of its post-2015 cases in 8.87 months on average. In that regard, Indonesia is recommended to seek to resolve the remaining 54% of the post-2015 cases pending on 31 December 2018 (34 cases) within a timeframe that results in an average timeframe of 24 months for all post-2015 cases.	
	[C.3]	Although MAP cases were closed within 24 months on average (which is the pursued average for resolving MAP cases received on or after 1 January 2016), peers indicated that they experienced several difficulties in resolving MAP cases, which concerns: • scheduling of face-to-face meetings • obtaining positions papers in due time (and before a face-to-face meeting) and with a substantial information on the case and an analysis and explanation of the competent authority's position • receiving responses to position papers issued by peers and receiving timely responses to communications on pending MAP cases. Therefore, there is a risk that pending post-2015 cases will in the future not be resolved within the pursued average of 24 months and this might indicate that the available resources for Indonesia's competent authority are not adequately used.	Indonesia should ensure that resources available for the competent authority function are adequately used in order to resolve MAP cases in a timely, efficient and effective manner. In this respect Indonesia should ensure that such adequate use enables its competent authority to: • more frequently hold face-to-face meetings • issue position papers in due time and include in those papers substantial information on the case and an analysis and explanation of the Indonesia's position • respond to position papers issued by competent authorities of the treaty partners and respond to communications on pending MAP cases with these partners in a timely manner. Furthermore, as Indonesia resolved attribution/allocation cases in 27.25 months on average, it could consider devoting current available resources to these cases in order to accelerate their resolution.
	[C.4]	-	As it has done thus far, Indonesia should continue to ensure that its competent authority has the authority, and uses that authority in practice, to resolve MAP cases without being dependent on approval or direction from the tax administration personnel directly involved in the adjustment at issue and absent any policy considerations that Indonesia would like to see reflected in future amendments to the treaty.
	[C.5]	-	As it has done thus far, Indonesia should continue to use appropriate performance indicators.
	[C.6]	No correct specification in the MAP profile on whether there are any legal limitations in its domestic law to include MAP arbitration in tax treaties.	Indonesia should correctly specify in its MAP profile whether there are any legal limitations in its domestic law to include MAP arbitration in tax treaties.

		Areas for improvement	Recommendations
		Part D: Implementation of MAP agreements	
[D.1]		As will be discussed under element D.3, not all of Indonesia's tax treaties contain the equivalent of Article 25(2), second sentence, of the OECD Model Tax Convention. Therefore, there is a risk that for those tax treaties that do not contain that provision, not all MAP agreements will be implemented due to time limits of five years in its domestic law. This regards only cases where the adjustment under review is made at the level of the treaty partner, while such is not the case for domestic adjustments.	When, after a MAP case is initiated, the domestic statute of limitation may, in the absence of the second sentence of Article 25(2) of the OECD Model Tax Convention in Indonesia's relevant tax treaty, prevent the implementation of a MAP agreement when the adjustment is made at the level of the treaty partner, Indonesia should put appropriate procedures in place to ensure that such an agreement is implemented. In addition, where during the MAP process the domestic statute of limitations may expire and may then affect the possibility to implement a MAP agreement, Indonesia should for clarity and transparency purposes notify the treaty partner thereof without delay.
[D.2]		-	As it has done thus far, Indonesia should continue to implement all MAP agreements on a timely basis if the conditions for such implementation are fulfilled.
[D.3]		52 out of 72 tax treaties contain neither a provision that is equivalent to Article 25(2), second sentence, of the OECD Model Tax Convention nor both alternative provisions provided for in Article 9(1) and Article 7(2). With respect to these 52 treaties: • 14 are expected to be modified by the Multilateral Instrument to include the required provision. • Nine are expected to be modified by the Multilateral Instrument to include the required provision, once the notifications under that instrument are modified.	Indonesia should as quickly as possible follow its stated intention and modify its notifications under the Multilateral Instrument and subsequently ratify that instrument to incorporate the equivalent to Article 25(2), second sentence, of the OECD Model Tax Convention in those 25 treaties that currently do not contain such equivalent and that will be modified by the Multilateral Instrument upon its entry into force for the treaties concerned. For 26 of the remaining 27 treaties that will not be modified by the Multilateral Instrument to include the equivalent of Article 25(2), second sentence, of the OECD Model Tax Convention, Indonesia should follow its stated intention to request the inclusion of the required provision via bilateral negotiations or be willing to accept the inclusion of both alternative provisions. To this end, Indonesia should put a plan in place on how it envisages updating these 26 treaties to include the required provision or its alternative. For the remaining treaty, Indonesia should enter into discussions with the relevant treaty partner following their invitations to open negotiations with a view to include such provision or both of alternative provisions.
			In addition, Indonesia should maintain its stated intention to include the required provision, or be willing to accept the inclusion of both alternatives provisions, in all future tax treaties.

Annex A

Tax treaty network of Indonesia

	Column 1	Column 2		Column 3	Column 4		Column 5	Column 6	Column 7	Column 8	Column 9	Column 10	Column 11
		DTC in force?		Article 25(1) of the OECD Model Tax Convention ("MTC")			Article 9(2) of the OECD MTC	Anti-abuse	Article 25(2) of the OECD MTC		Article 25(3) of the OECD MTC		Arbitration
				B.1	B.1		B.3	B.4	C.1	D.3	A.1	B.7	C.6
	Treaty partner	Y = yes, N = signed pending ratification	If N, date of signing	Inclusion Art. 25(1) first sentence? — If yes, submission to either competent authority? (new Art. 25(1), first sentence) E = yes, either CAs; O = yes, only one CA; N = No	Inclusion Art. 25(1) second sentence? (Note 1) — If no, please state reasons: Y = yes; i = no, no such provision; ii = no, different period; iii = no, starting point for computing the 3 year period is different; iv = no, other reasons	if ii, specify period	Inclusion Art. 9(2) (Note 2) If no, will your CA provide access to MAP in TP cases? Y = yes; i = no, but access will be given to TP cases; ii = no and access will not be given to TP cases	Inclusion provision that MAP Article will not be available in cases where your jurisdiction is of the assessment that there is an abuse of the DTC or of the domestic tax law? If no, will your CA accept a taxpayer's request for MAP in relation to such cases? Y = yes; i = no and such cases will be accepted for MAP; ii = no but such cases will not be accepted for MAP	Inclusion Art. 25(2) first sentence? (Note 3) Y = yes; N = no	Inclusion Art. 25(2) second sentence? (Note 4) If no, alternative provision in Art. 7 & 9 OECD MTC? (Note 4) Y = yes; i = no, but have Art. 7 equivalent; ii = no, but have Art. 9 equivalent; iii = no, but have both Art. 7 & 9 equivalent; N = no and no equivalent of Art. 7 and 9	Inclusion Art. 25(3) first sentence? (Note 5) Y = yes; N = no	Inclusion Art. 25(3) second sentence? (Note 6) Y = yes; N = no	Inclusion arbitration provision? Y = yes; N = no
	Algeria	Y	N/A	O	ii	2-years	Y	i	Y	N	Y	Y	N
	Armenia	Y	N/A	O	Y	N/A	Y	i	Y	N	Y	Y	N
	Australia	Y	N/A	O	Y	N/A	Y	i	Y	Y	N	N	N
	Austria	Y	N/A	N	ii	2-years	i	i	Y	N	Y	Y	N

Treaty partner (Column 1)	DTC in force? (Column 2)		Inclusion Art. 25(1) first sentence? — B.1 (Column 3)	If yes, submission to either competent authority? (new Art. 25(1), first sentence)	Inclusion Art. 25(1) second sentence? (Note 1) / If no, please state reasons — B.1 (Column 4)	Inclusion Art. 9(2) (Note 2) If no, will your CA provide access to MAP in TP cases? — B.3 (Column 5)	If no, will your CA accept a taxpayer's request for MAP in relation to such cases? — B.4 (Column 6)	Inclusion Art. 25(2) first sentence? (Note 3) — C.1 (Column 7)	If no, alternative provision in Art. 7 & 9 OECD MTC? (Note 4) — D.3 (Column 8)	Inclusion Art. 25(3) first sentence? (Note 5) — A.1 (Column 9)	Inclusion Art. 25(3) second sentence? (Note 6) — B.7 (Column 10)	Inclusion arbitration provision? — C.6 (Column 11)
Bangladesh	Y	N/A	O	N/A	Y	Y	i	Y	Y	Y	Y	N
Belarus	Y	N/A	O	N/A	Y	Y	i	Y	N	Y	Y	N
Belgium	Y	N/A	O	N/A	Y	i	i	Y	N*	Y	N*	N
Brunei	Y	N/A	O	N/A	Y	Y	i	Y	N	Y	Y	N
Bulgaria	Y	N/A	O	2-years	ii	i	i	Y	N	Y	Y	N
Cambodia	N	13/10/2017	O	N/A	Y	Y	i	Y	N	Y	Y	N
Canada	Y	N/A	O	2-years	ii*	i	i	Y	iii	Y	Y	N
China (People's Republic of)	Y	N/A	O	N/A	Y	Y	i	Y	N*	Y	N	N
Croatia	Y	N/A	O	N/A	Y	Y	i	Y	N*	Y	Y	N
Czech Republic	Y	N/A	O	N/A	i	i	i	Y	N	Y	Y	N
Denmark	Y	N/A	O	N/A	Y	Y	i	Y	Y	Y	Y	N
Egypt	Y	N/A	O	2-years	iii	Y	i	Y	iii	Y	N	N
Finland	Y	N/A	O	N/A	Y	Y	i	Y	Y	Y	Y	N
France	Y	N/A	O	N/A	Y	i	i	Y	N*	N	Y	N
Germany	Y	N/A	O	2-years	iii	i	i	Y	Y	Y	Y	N
Hong Kong (China)	Y	N/A	O	N/A	Y	Y	i	Y	Y	Y	Y	N
Hungary	Y	N/A	O	2-years	iii	i	i	Y	Y	Y	Y	N

Treaty partner (Column 1)	DTC in force? (Column 2)		Article 25(1) of the OECD Model Tax Convention ("MTC")			Article 9(2) of the OECD MTC (Column 5)	Anti-abuse (Column 6)	Article 25(2) of the OECD MTC		Article 25(3) of the OECD MTC		Arbitration (Column 11)
			B.1 Inclusion Art. 25(1) first sentence? (Column 3)	B.1 Inclusion Art. 25(1) second sentence? (Note 1) — If yes, submission to either competent authority? (new Art. 25(1), first sentence) (Column 4)	If no, please state reasons	B.3 Inclusion Art. 9(2) (Note 2) If no, will your CA provide access to MAP in TP cases?	B.4 Inclusion provision that MAP Article will not be available in cases where your jurisdiction is of the assessment that there is an abuse of the DTC or of the domestic tax law? — If no, will your CA accept a taxpayer's request for MAP in relation to such cases?	C.1 Inclusion Art. 25(2) first sentence? (Note 3) (Column 7)	D.3 If no, alternative provision in Art. 7 & 9 OECD MTC? (Note 4) / Inclusion Art. 25(2) second sentence? (Note 4) (Column 8)	A.1 Inclusion Art. 25(3) first sentence? (Note 5) (Column 9)	B.7 Inclusion Art. 25(3) second sentence? (Note 6) (Column 10)	C.6 Inclusion arbitration provision?
India	Y	N/A	O	Y	N/A	Y	i	Y	Y	Y	Y	N
Iran	Y	N/A	O	ii	2-years	Y	i	Y	N	Y	Y	N
Italy	Y	N/A	N	ii*	2-years	i	i	Y	N*	Y	N	N
Japan	Y	N/A	O	Y	N/A	i	i	Y	Y	Y	Y	N
Jordan	Y	N/A	O	ii	2-years	Y	i	Y	N	Y	Y	N
Korea	Y	N/A	O	Y	N/A	Y	i	Y	Y	Y	Y	N
Korea (Democratic People's Republic of)	Y	N/A	O	ii	2-years	Y	i	Y	N	Y	Y	N
Kuwait	Y	N/A	O	Y	N/A	Y	i	Y	N	Y	Y	N
Laos	Y	N/A	O	Y	N/A	Y	i	Y	Y	Y	Y	N
Luxembourg	Y	N/A	O	ii*	2-years	Y	i	Y	N*	Y	Y	N
Malaysia	Y	N/A	O	Y	N/A	i	i	Y	N*	Y	Y	Y
Mexico	Y	N/A	O	i	N/A	i	i	N	N	Y	Y	N
Mongolia	Y	N/A	O	Y	N/A	Y	i	Y	N	Y	Y	N
Morocco	Y	N/A	O	Y	N/A	Y	i	Y	N	Y	Y	N
Myanmar	N	1/4/2003	O	Y	N/A	Y	i	Y	N	Y	Y	N
Netherlands	Y	N/A	O	Y	N/A	Y	i	Y	N*	Y	Y	N

Treaty partner	DTC in force?	Inclusion Art. 25(1) first sentence? / If yes, submission to either competent authority? (new Art. 25(1), first sentence)	Inclusion Art. 25(1) second sentence? (Note 1)	If no, please state reasons	Inclusion Art. 9(2) (Note 2) If no, will your CA provide access to MAP in TP cases?	Inclusion provision that MAP Article will not be available in cases where your jurisdiction is of the assessment that there is an abuse of the DTC or of the domestic tax law? / If no, will your CA accept a taxpayer's request for MAP in relation to such cases?	Inclusion Art. 25(2) first sentence? (Note 3)	If no, alternative provision in Art. 7 & 9 OECD MTC? (Note 4)	Inclusion Art. 25(3) first sentence? (Note 5)	Inclusion Art. 25(3) second sentence? (Note 6)	Inclusion arbitration provision?
	Column 2	Column 3 (B.1)	Column 4 (B.1)		Column 5 (B.3)	Column 6 (B.4)	Column 7 (C.1)	Column 8 (D.3)	Column 9 (A.1)	Column 10 (B.7)	Column 11 (C.6)
New Zealand	Y	N/A	O	ii*	2-years	i	i	Y	N*	Y	Y	N
Norway	Y	N/A	O	Y	N/A	i	i	Y	Y	Y	Y	N
Pakistan	Y	N/A	O	ii	2-years	Y	i	Y	Y	Y	Y	N
Papua New Guinea	Y	N/A	O	Y	N/A	Y	i	Y	N	Y	Y	N
Philippines	Y	N/A	O	ii	2-years	Y	i	Y	iii	Y	Y	N
Poland	Y	N/A	O	ii*	2-years	Y	i	Y	N*	Y	Y	N
Portugal	Y	N/A	O	ii	2-years	i	i	Y	N	Y	Y	N
Qatar	Y	N/A	O	ii*	2-years	Y	i	Y	N	Y	Y	N
Romania	Y	N/A	O	ii	2-years	i	i	Y	N	Y	Y	N
Russia	Y	N/A	O	ii	2-years	i	i	Y	N	Y	Y	N
Serbia	Y	N/A	O	ii	2-years	Y	i	Y	ii	Y	Y	N
Seychelles	Y	N/A	O	ii*	2-years	Y	i	Y	N*	Y	Y	N
Singapore	Y	N/A	O	Y	N/A	i	i	Y	Y	Y	Y	N
Slovak Republic	Y	N/A	O	Y	N/A	Y	i	Y	N	Y	Y	N
South Africa	Y	N/A	O	ii*	2-years	i	i	Y	N	Y	Y	N
Spain	Y	N/A	O	ii	2-years	i	i	Y	N	Y	Y	N
Sri Lanka	Y	N/A	O	ii	2-years	Y	i	Y	N	Y	Y	N
Sudan	Y	N/A	O	ii	2-years	Y	i	Y	N	Y	Y	N

Column 1	Column 2		Column 3	Column 4		Column 5	Column 6	Column 7	Column 8	Column 9	Column 10	Column 11
			Article 25(1) of the OECD Model Tax Convention ("MTC")			Article 9(2) of the OECD MTC	Anti-abuse	Article 25(2) of the OECD MTC		Article 25(3) of the OECD MTC		Arbitration
			B.1	B.1		B.3	B.4	C.1	D.3	A.1	B.7	C.6
Treaty partner	DTC in force?		Inclusion Art. 25(1) first sentence?	If yes, submission to either competent authority? (new Art. 25(1), first sentence) / Inclusion Art. 25(1) second sentence? (Note 1)	If no, please state reasons	Inclusion Art. 9(2) (Note 2) If no, will your CA provide access to MAP in TP cases?	Inclusion provision that MAP Article will not be available in cases where your jurisdiction is of the assessment that there is an abuse of the DTC or of the domestic tax law? / If no, will your CA accept a taxpayer's request for MAP in relation to such cases?	Inclusion Art. 25(2) first sentence? (Note 3)	Inclusion Art. 25(2) second sentence? (Note 4) / If no, alternative provision in Art. 7 & 9 OECD MTC? (Note 4)	Inclusion Art. 25(3) first sentence? (Note 5)	Inclusion Art. 25(3) second sentence? (Note 6)	Inclusion arbitration provision?
Suriname	Y	N/A	O	ii	2-years	Y	i	Y	N	Y	Y	N
Sweden	Y	N/A	O	Y	N/A	Y	i	Y	Y	Y	Y	N
Switzerland	Y	N/A	O	ii	2-years	i	i	Y	N	Y	Y	N
Syrian Arab Republic	Y	N/A	O	ii	2-years	Y	i	Y	N	Y	Y	N
Chinese Taipei	Y	N/A	O	Y	N/A	Y	i	Y	N	Y	Y	N
Tajikistan	N	28/10/2003	O	ii	2-years	Y	i	Y	N	Y	Y	N
Thailand	Y	N/A	O	ii	2-years	i	i	Y	N	Y	Y	N
Tunisia	Y	N/A	O	Y	N/A	i	i	Y	N	Y	Y	N
Turkey	Y	N/A	O	i	N/A	Y	i	Y	N*	Y	Y	N
Ukraine	Y	N/A	O	ii	2-years	Y	i	Y	N	Y	Y	N
United Arab Emirates	Y	N/A	O	ii*	2-years	Y	i	Y	N*	Y	Y	N
United Kingdom	Y	N/A	O	i	N/A	i	i	Y	N*	Y	N*	N
United States	Y	N/A	O	Y	N/A	Y	i	Y	Y	N	Y	N
Uzbekistan	Y	N/A	O	Y	N/A	Y	i	Y	N	Y	Y	N
Venezuela	Y	N/A	O	Y	N/A	i	i	Y	N	Y	Y	N
Viet Nam	Y	N/A	O	Y	N/A	Y	i	Y	N	Y	Y	N
Zimbabwe	N	30/5/2001	O	Y	N/A	Y	i	Y	N	Y	Y	N

Legend:

E* The provision contained in this treaty was already in line with the requirements under this element of the Action 14 Minimum Standard, but has been modified by the Multilateral Instrument to allow the filing of a MAP request in either contracting state.

E** The provision contained in this treaty was not in line with the requirements under this element of the Action 14 Minimum Standard, but the treaty has been modified by the Multilateral Instrument and is now in line with this standard.

O* The provision contained in this treaty is already in line with the requirements under this element of the Action 14 Minimum Standard, but will be modified by the Multilateral Instrument upon entry into force for this specific treaty and will then allow the filing of a MAP request in either contracting state.

Y* The provision contained in this treaty was not in line with the requirements under this element of the Action 14 Minimum Standard, but the treaty has been modified by the Multilateral Instrument and is now in line with this element of the Action 14 Minimum Standard.

Y** The provision contained in this treaty already included an arbitration provision, which has been replaced by part VI of the Multilateral Instrument containing a mandatory and binding arbitration procedure.

Y*** The provision contained in this treaty did not include an arbitration provision, but part VI of the Multilateral Instrument applies, following which a mandatory and binding arbitration procedure is included in this treaty

i*/ii*/iv*/N* The provision contained in this treaty is not in line with the requirements under this element of the Action 14 Minimum Standard, but the treaty will be modified by the Multilateral Instrument upon entry into force for this specific treaty and will then be in line with this element of the Action 14 Minimum Standard.

i**/iv**/N** The provision contained in this treaty is not in line with the requirements under this element of the Action 14 Minimum Standard, but the treaty will be superseded by the Multilateral Instrument upon entry into force for this specific treaty only to the extent that existing treaty provisions are incompatible with the relevant provision of the Multilateral Instrument.

i*** The provision contained in this treaty is not in line with the requirements under this element of the Action 14 Minimum Standard, but the treaty will be superseded by the Multilateral Instrument only to the extent that existing treaty provisions are incompatible with the relevant provision of the Multilateral Instrument.

Annex B

MAP Statistics Reporting for pre-2016 cases

2016 MAP Statistics

Category of cases	No. of pre-2016 cases in MAP inventory on 1 January 2016	Number of pre-2016 cases closed during the reporting period by outcome										No. of pre-2016 cases remaining in on MAP inventory on 31 December 2016	Average time taken (in months) for closing pre-2016 cases during the reporting period
		Denied MAP access	Objection is not justified	Withdrawn by taxpayer	Unilateral relief granted	Resolved via domestic remedy	Agreement fully eliminating double taxation/fully resolving taxation not in accordance with tax treaty	Agreement partially eliminating double taxation/partially resolving taxation not in accordance with tax treaty	Agreement that there is no taxation not in accordance with tax treaty	No agreement, including agreement to disagree	Any other outcome		
Column 1	Column 2	Column 3	Column 4	Column 5	Column 6	Column 7	Column 8	Column 9	Column 10	Column 11	Column 12	Column 13	Column 14
Attribution/ Allocation	23	0	0	0	0	2	2	1	0	0	0	18	39.98
Others	45	0	0	0	1	0	0	0	0	0	26	18	27.90
Total	68	0	0	0	1	2	2	1	0	0	26	36	29.78

Notes: The numbers of cases in the inventory are different from those in Indonesia's published MAP statistics. This results from the reclassification of cases and late notification of cases from other treaty partners.

2017 MAP Statistics

Category of cases	No. of pre-2016 cases in MAP inventory on 1 January 2017	Number of pre-2016 cases closed during the reporting period by outcome										No. of pre-2016 cases remaining in on MAP inventory on 31 December 2017	Average time taken (in months) for closing pre-2016 cases during the reporting period
		Denied MAP access	Objection is not justified	Withdrawn by taxpayer	Unilateral relief granted	Resolved via domestic remedy	Agreement fully eliminating double taxation/fully resolving taxation not in accordance with tax treaty	Agreement partially eliminating double taxation/partially resolving taxation not in accordance with tax treaty	Agreement that there is no taxation not in accordance with tax treaty	No agreement, including agreement to disagree	Any other outcome		
Column 1	Column 2	Column 3	Column 4	Column 5	Column 6	Column 7	Column 8	Column 9	Column 10	Column 11	Column 12	Column 13	Column 14
Attribution/ Allocation	18	0	0	0	0	2	1	0	0	1	0	14	42.21
Others	18	0	0	0	0	0	2	0	0	1	0	15	51.36
Total	36	0	0	0	0	2	3	0	0	2	0	29	46.13

2018 MAP Statistics

Category of cases	No. of pre-2016 cases in MAP inventory on 1 January 2018	Number of pre-2016 cases closed during the reporting period by outcome											No. of pre-2016 cases remaining in on MAP inventory on 31 December 2018	Average time taken (in months) for closing pre-2016 cases during the reporting period
		Denied MAP access	Objection is not justified	Withdrawn by taxpayer	Unilateral relief granted	Resolved via domestic remedy	Agreement fully eliminating double taxation/fully resolving taxation not in accordance with tax treaty	Agreement partially eliminating double taxation/partially resolving taxation not in accordance with tax treaty	Agreement that there is no taxation not in accordance with tax treaty	No agreement, including agreement to disagree	Any other outcome		
Column 1	Column 2	Column 3	Column 4	Column 5	Column 6	Column 7	Column 8	Column 9	Column 10	Column 11	Column 12	Column 13	Column 14
Attribution/ Allocation	14	0	0	0	0	0	4	0	0	0	0	10	48.78
Others	15	0	0	0	0	0	0	0	0	0	0	15	0.00
Total	29	0	0	0	0	0	4	0	0	0	0	25	48.78

Annex C

MAP Statistics Reporting for post-2015 cases

2016 MAP Statistics

Category of cases	No. of post-2015 cases in MAP inventory on 1 January 2016	No. of post-2015 cases started during the reporting period	Number of post-2015 cases closed during the reporting period by outcome										No. of post-2015 cases remaining in on MAP inventory on 31 December 2016	Average time taken (in months) for closing post-2015 cases during the reporting period
			Denied MAP access	Objection is not justified	Withdrawn by taxpayer	Unilateral relief granted	Resolved via domestic remedy	Agreement fully eliminating double taxation/fully resolving taxation not in accordance with tax treaty	Agreement partially eliminating double taxation/partially resolving taxation not in accordance with tax treaty	Agreement that there is no taxation not in accordance with tax treaty	No agreement, including agreement to disagree	Any other outcome		
Column 1	Column 2	Column 3	Column 4	Column 5	Column 6	Column 7	Column 8	Column 9	Column 10	Column 11	Column 12	Column 13	Column 14	Column 15
Attribution/ Allocation	0	9	0	0	0	0	0	0	0	0	0	0	9	N/A
Others	0	10	0	0	0	0	0	0	0	0	0	0	10	N/A
Total	0	19	0	0	0	0	0	0	0	0	0	0	19	N/A

2017 MAP Statistics

Category of cases	No. of post-2015 cases in MAP inventory on 1 January 2017	No. of post-2015 cases started during the reporting period	Number of post-2015 cases closed during the reporting period by outcome										No. of post-2015 cases remaining in on MAP inventory on 31 December 2017	Average time taken (in months) for closing post-2015 cases during the reporting period
			Denied MAP access	Objection is not justified	Withdrawn by taxpayer	Unilateral relief granted	Resolved via domestic remedy	Agreement fully eliminating double taxation/fully resolving taxation not in accordance with tax treaty	Agreement partially eliminating double taxation/partially resolving taxation not in accordance with tax treaty	Agreement that there is no taxation not in accordance with tax treaty	No agreement, including agreement to disagree	Any other outcome		
Column 1	Column 2	Column 3	Column 4	Column 5	Column 6	Column 7	Column 8	Column 9	Column 10	Column 11	Column 12	Column 13	Column 14	Column 15
Attribution/ Allocation	9	13	0	0	1	0	0	2	0	0	0	0	19	16.14
Others	10	5	0	0	0	0	2	0	4	1	2	2	4	9.38
Total	19	18	0	0	1	0	2	2	4	1	2	2	23	10.83

Notes: The numbers of cases in the inventory are different from those in Indonesia's published MAP statistics. This results from the reclassification of cases and late notification of cases from other treaty partners.

2018 MAP Statistics

Category of cases	No. of post-2015 cases in MAP inventory on 1 January 2018	No. of post-2015 cases started during the reporting period	Number of post-2015 cases closed during the reporting period by outcome										No. of post-2015 cases remaining in on MAP inventory on 31 December 2018	Average time taken (in months) for closing post-2015 cases during the reporting period
			Denied MAP access	Objection is not justified	Withdrawn by taxpayer	Unilateral relief granted	Resolved via domestic remedy	Agreement fully eliminating double taxation/fully resolving taxation not in accordance with tax treaty	Agreement partially eliminating double taxation/partially resolving taxation not in accordance with tax treaty	Agreement that there is no taxation not in accordance with tax treaty	No agreement, including agreement to disagree	Any other outcome		
Column 1	Column 2	Column 3	Column 4	Column 5	Column 6	Column 7	Column 8	Column 9	Column 10	Column 11	Column 12	Column 13	Column 14	Column 15
Attribution/ Allocation	19	18	0	0	2	0	1	4	0	0	3	0	27	9.62
Others	4	8	0	0	0	1	0	4	0	0	0	0	7	1.91
Total	23	26	0	0	2	1	1	8	0	0	3	0	34	7.05

Glossary

Action 14 Minimum Standard	The minimum standard as agreed upon in the final report on Action 14: Making Dispute Resolution Mechanisms More Effective
MAP Guidance	Regulation of Minister of Finance No. 240/PMK.03/2014 concerning the Implementation Guidelines of Mutual Agreement Procedure
MAP Statistics Reporting Framework	Rules for reporting of MAP statistics as agreed by the FTA MAP Forum
Multilateral Instrument	Multilateral Convention to Implement Tax Treaty Related Measures to Prevent Base Erosion and Profit Shifting
OECD Model Tax Convention	OECD Model Tax Convention on Income and on Capital as it read on 21 November 2017
OECD Transfer Pricing Guidelines	OECD Transfer Pricing Guidelines for Multinational Enterprises and Tax Administrations
Pre-2016 cases	MAP cases in a competent authority's inventory that are pending resolution on 31 December 2015
Post-2015 cases	MAP cases that are received by a competent authority from the taxpayer on or after 1 January 2016
Review Period	Period for the peer review process that started on 1 January 2016 and ended on 31 December 2018
Statistics Reporting Period	Period for reporting MAP statistics that started on 1 January 2016 and that ended on 31 December 2018
Terms of Reference	Terms of reference to monitor and review the implementing of the BEPS Action 14 Minimum Standard to make dispute resolution mechanisms more effective

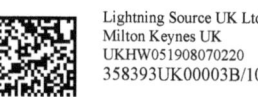